# How to Personally Profit From the Laws of Success

By Sterling W. Sill

The National Institute of Financial Planning, Inc.
Salt Lake City, Utah

6th Printing, 1981

Published and distributed by
The National Institute of Financial Planning, Inc.
Salt Lake City, Utah

# CONTENTS

# HOW TO READ THIS BOOK

At the end of each chapter, there is at least one blank page entitled "Plans and Goals." These blank pages are for you to write your thoughts, ideas, and goals. Do not write my thoughts; write the thoughts that are stimulated in your mind from reading my comments.

You will find as you read this book, particularly the second and third time, that your own ideas multiply. Consequently, you will find yourself writing many of your own great thoughts.

My task is not only to show you the laws and methods that will lead you to success, but also to stimulate your mind and bring out great thoughts and ideas that are and always have been in your mind. Those thoughts, along with a little direction and guidance that will help you form a game plan, will bring rewards and riches you once thought came only to others.

# A SUCCESS LAW IS . . .
## Success Theory Practiced and Proven

As a rule we can achieve success by the application of the same principles other successful people use. These principles are easily available to all of us, yet we sometimes envy others their wealth and success without ever thinking of studying their philosophy and appropriating it for our own use.

We may look at a person in the hour of his triumph and think of him as a "born" success. We overlook the importance of analyzing his methods, and we forget the price he had to pay and is paying in careful, well-organized preparation.

A law is a theory practiced and proven. The laws of success contained in this book have come to us because of the many before us who have applied success theory until they established consistent success law.

How can you personally profit from these laws of success? First, arrange for regular periods of solitude where you can concentrate and indulge your imagination without distraction. Then study and ponder the material in the following pages. Make specific plans and set goals. Become well organized and prepared. If you do these things, along with *practicing and re-proving* these success laws for yourself, you will indeed become the successful person you were born to be.

# 1
# The Law of
# ABUNDANCE

Suppose you had a son whom you loved very much and that you had surrounded him with every opportunity and all good things. He could have all the education he wished. Medical knowledge is available which, if heeded, would give him a strong body and a clear mind. He could develop personality, courage, industry, and leadership to his heart's content. All of the best things would be available to him in the greatest abundance. Can you conceive of placing any limit on him as long as this abundance was in his interest?

With all of these opportunities, suppose your son showed himself to be unworthy, unkept, without education, without personality, without vision or understanding, half-starved physically, mentally, and spiritually. How would you feel?

## The Abundance of Nature

Isn't that just about our situation? Think of the lavish abundance with which creation surrounds us. Everything we could possibly wish for has been placed within our easy reach. It was certainly intended that everyone who wished it should have an abundance. There is enough and to spare. There is sufficient electricity in the water of a creek to furnish the equivalent power of a million slaves. There is enough atomic energy in the substance we could hold in one hand to light the world. If every person produced to his utmost and we did away with strikes, monopolies, crime, and waste, everyone could have his needs supplied many times over. Think of the lavishness of our natural resources: land, water, solar power, air, iron, coal deposits, and forests. Think also of the resources in our own personality that lie buried and mostly unused.

Nature gives us everything in abundance and expects us to manifest that abundance in our lives. The Creator did not intend us to be scrubs, and certainly that is not the example that he sets for us. Only one millionth part of the sun's rays reach our planet to maintain life; the rest of its beams travel in cold, empty space and encounter nothing to reflect heat and light. Think of the order, the efficiency, the regularity and dependability of the workings of the universe. Try to contemplate the efficiency and attitude of the mind that could produce such order and abundance. Do you suppose that the mind that brought into being worlds without number and all the wealth of creation intends us, his children, to be scrawny, uneducated, and underfed, deprived of the few things necessary to our happiness, or that he intends us to live in want, sickness, fear, ignorance, and insecurity?

Jesus said, "And all things, whatsoever ye shall ask in prayer, believing, ye shall receive." (Matthew 21:22.) "Give, and it shall be given unto you; good measure, pressed down, and shaken together, and running over. . . ." (Luke 6:38.)

There are no signs of any limitation mentioned here.

Think how lavishly nature rewards us for the things we do in a material way. If we plant one bushel of seed potatoes in the ground, we can get back sixty bushels of potatoes in return. A single potato carried to England by Sir Walter Raleigh in the sixteenth century multiplied itself into food for millions. A single tomato seed can multiply itself a million times in one year. Ten forests can come out of one acorn. Plant a pound of onion seed and we may reap ten tons of onions. One twig from an apple tree planted in the ground may become a great tree, producing foliage and blossoms and fragrance and fruit not just for one year, but for many years. The two eggs that we intend to eat for breakfast tomorrow morning could be hatched into a pair of fowls and multiplied to cover the earth with poultry.

## The Mustard Seed Principle

Is it likely we would be rewarded less in other areas of life? A little investment in character pays us back a million-fold. Every pound of energy we put into education for the development of initiative, resourcefulness, courage, industry, and personality, we get back multiplied manyfold. For every manifestation of faith as a grain of mustard seed, we are told we can move mountains; every determination that we put into life comes back to us fantastically multiplied.

*Nature is rich, and it was intended that every man, woman, and child should be rich likewise.* To be in want is a sin. Plutarch said that while poverty may not be dishonorable in itself, it is usually the manifestation of laziness, intemperance, carelessness, lack of planning, and lack of courage. In contrast, upon a person who is temperate, industrious, just, and valiant and who uses all of his virtues and develops a great, lofty mind and an active body, fortune will pour her whole cornucopia of wealth, honor, and worldly goods.

The essence of the law of abundance is that we must believe in abundance. We must think abundance. We must raise our sights for greater accomplishments and let no thought of failure or limitation enter our minds. We must think success and feel success and work for success. Our boundaries should be expanded. *"Man was intended to be rich,"* said Emerson.

Most of us tend to underrate our own dignity, importance, and potentiality. It was certainly not intended that we live as slaves, beggars, or vagrants. There is no such thing as lack of opportunity. The important thing is to believe and then take the first step. Just to begin is to complete the first half of the job. Then if we work toward the goal with all our hearts, why should failure even be thought of ? It was never intended that we should be poor or worried or unable to pay our bills when we are surrounded with an abundance which is ours for the asking.

But when we think fear and discouragement and failure, that's what we get. To take advantage of the law of abundance, we must think strength, think health, think riches. Our achievements today are but the sum total of our thoughts of yesterday. Whatever price we set upon ourselves, life will give it to us. If we visualize and emphasize our worries, our fears, and our negative attitudes, we live with and become saturated by them. We make them real by our practice of failure. If we control our thoughts, we can control our circumstances. There is scarcely a poor person who was not made poor by his own shortcomings or by the shortcomings of someone else. It is all wrong to be poor anyway.

Overcoming Obstacles

We often see potentially great salesmen who give many reasons why they cannot succeed. They think they have a lack of ability, or they are worried because of finances. They fill their minds with negative thoughts. How foolish and shortsighted is such counsel! In the first place, it is not true. Most of the great accomplishments in the world have been made under tremendous difficulty.

Both Caesar and Napoleon were epileptics at the very time in their lives when they were making themselves the most powerful. Many people who are presently drawing disability benefits are in better shape than Julius Caesar was while he was conquering the world. John Milton wrote *Paradise Lost,* one of the world's greatest pieces of literature, while he was totally blind and living in complete poverty. George Washington won the American Revolution while many influences were working against him, and in spite of Valley Forge, where his soldiers went barefoot in the snow, without food and without equipment. Abraham Lincoln had to borrow money for his railroad ticket to go to Washington to give his inaugural address. What would have happened if in his poverty he had said, "I can't work because I'm worried"? He had no money, no possessions, few opportunities; yet he raised himself to be one of our greatest presidents because he thought positively and kept trying.

We should be very careful about what we think, because that's what we become. If we think we can't, we can't; if we think failure, we fail. On the other hand, persons of faith and vision usually do their best work when they know there is no retreat. They decide to fight instead of run, and that is a great moment in anyone's life. Necessity is still the mother of invention, but it is more than that. It builds desire and determination, and it develops vision. There is no incentive like necessity. A determined purpose cannot be stopped. The more you dam it, the more power is accumulated behind the dam, until it eventually sweeps everything before it. Nothing can stop us if we only believe. Walt Whitman said, "Nothing external to me has any power over me."

The only time we get into trouble is when we start to whine and cringe and alibi and say, "I can't work or believe because ..." We allow ourselves to think negatively about competition and hard times; we allow our fears and worries to undermine our confidence; and we fail to reach out and help ourselves to the abundance with which we are surrounded.

Magnetic Thinking

Thoughts are energy; thoughts are magnets that attract to us the various things we think. The greatest shortcut to prosperity is to believe in it. Prosperity attracts; poverty repels. This is the operation of the law which says, "For whosoever hath, to him shall be given, and he shall have more abundance: but whosoever hath not, from him shall be taken away even that he hath." (Matthew 13:12.)

In one way, failure is like success. Both are "inside" jobs. People live in poverty and want because they are so wrapped up in their suffering that they give out thoughts of poverty and unhappiness. Thoughts attract in kind, and when we think poverty, nothing else is possible. All of our lives we have known in a vague sort of way that developing our faith, like getting money, is the result of earning it, but most of us never get a very good vision of that very powerful idea. Summed up, the result of all experience is that man gets back in kind what he gives out, except it is multiplied. If you work twice as hard and twice as smart as the guy next to you, eventually you will earn not twice as much, but ten times or more.

Many of us have eyes but don't see the great opportunities that are staring us in the face. The poor fellow who said, "I hid my talent in the ground and have earned nothing," was not only afraid, he was blind. Of course, the first and all-important thing is that we must know what we want. Before we can have our heart's desire, we must get clearly fixed in our mind's eye what we want and then concentrate all our attention on that one thing. Most of us struggle on in a vague sort of way, hoping that something may turn up, not knowing definitely what we expect. We usually waste enough energy to get us to our destination — if we only knew where we wanted to go. But like a drowning man, we fritter away our strength in futile struggle, threshing the air without direction, exhausting ourselves without getting anywhere. Most of us spend far more energy on the detours than on the main line.

Remember that nature is rich, and Creation intends that all shall have an abundance, good measure, pressed down, shaken together, filled up, and running over. All we need to do is obey the law of abundance.

> I bargained with life for a penny,
> Only to find dismayed
> That anything I had asked of life,
> Life would have paid.

Place in your mind, after careful thought, exactly what you want. Try to be specific (like double your salary within twelve months). Now, concentrate with all your time and energy on that goal. Do this everyday while you study and think of specific ways to achieve your objective. Do this along with the application of the other Laws in this book and you will accomplish all of your objectives and gain a huge share of the great abundance this life has to offer.

In the following chapter you will see how one very common man did this.

# Plans and Goals

# 2
# The Law of
# BELIEVING IN YOURSELF

In 1912, Harry Leon Wilson wrote a novel of some 300 pages entitled *Bunker Bean*. It is an intriguing story about a man who was tricked into believing in himself.

Most people suffer throughout life from too mean an estimate of their own abilities. Consequently they spend their strength on small tasks and never put their real powers fairly to trial.

The experience of Bunker Bean makes the potential power of believing more clearly visible. There is a part of our literature that comes under the heading of 'useful fiction.' Throughout all history the myth, the fable, the allegory, the novel have been used with great effectiveness to teach principles. A remarkable thing about a parable is that it does not need to be true as an actual occurrence. It is of far greater importance that the truths it teaches and the principles it illustrates are true and clearly recognizable. In the parables of the Bible many of life's vital experiences are captured and their messages made timeless with a universal application.

Bunker Bean's parents died when he was but a child, and he was left alone in the world. He 'roamed the earth in rags and lived timidly through its terrors.' Because he was inferior many of his friends made fun of him. *And his mind was full of fears.* He was afraid of policemen; he was afraid to ride in the elevator, as each time the elevator seemed to fall he suffered the sensations of dying. He was afraid of the future, afraid of situations, afraid of things, afraid of life — even afraid of himself.

Then one day a false spiritualistic medium moved into the cheap boarding-house where Bunker Bean lived. This man had a book on reincarnation, and he persuaded young Bunker Bean to believe that as we cast off our worn-out shoes and replace them with new, so we cast off our worn-out bodies and reclothe our spirits by this process of reincarnation.

Bunker Bean believed wholeheartedly in the teaching of his new-found friend. He was convinced that the friend possessed some extraordinary powers given to him from another world. This man persuaded Bunker Bean that in return for his savings and a part of his wages over a long period, he could tell him about his (Bunker Bean's) previous incarnations.

After a considerable delay and seemingly with great effort on the part of the medium, Bunker Bean was surprised and delighted to learn that he, the weak, timid Bunker Bean, had once been the great Napoleon Bonaparte, the master of the world. It was quite a shock to learn that once people had been afraid of *him*. When he had been Napoleon the world had trembled before him. Then policemen had been to him as insects.

This he could not understand, and so he inquired of his friend why it was that Napoleon had been so courageous and Bunker Bean so timid. The medium explained that life went in vast karmic cycles. Napoleon had lived on the upper half of the cycle when the qualities of courage, initiative and power had been in the ascendancy. But Bunker Bean lived in the lower part of the cycle that was characterized by timidity, fear and weakness. Therefore Bunker Bean possessed the exact opposites of the great Napoleonic courage and self-confidence.

## The Cycle Renewed

But there was some wonderful news awaiting Bunker Bean. He was told by his friend that the lower part of the cycle was just now being completed and he was re-entering that period in which he had lived so famously as Napoleon the Great. He was assured that it would not be many days before he himself would know this truth. He would soon feel a strange life stirring within him, for he was even now well on the way to becoming his own inspired, courageous, determined self again — strong, self-reliant, fearless and successful.

Even the *thought* of who he really was made Bunker Bean expand his chest. He straightened his shoulders and studied himself in the glass. Now that he thought about it, there was a certain majesty in his look. The thought of who he was and of his former accomplishments made him vibrate with a strange, fresh power never known before. *He went to the library, where he secured and enthusiastically read every book about Napoleon, his former self.* He devoured every idea and absorbed the ambition of the mighty Bonaparte, for he, Bunker Bean, was now determined to prepare himself to give full play to those great qualities which were beginning to reappear in his life. At all costs he must learn immediately the secrets that had previously brought him such overwhelming success.

He collected pictures of Napoleon and hung them around his little attic room where he could feast his mind upon them. He imitated the speech, thoughts and acts of his former self. He *was* about the same height as Napoleon, and he now remembered for the first time that he did possess some of those qualities of character that had distinguished the great general.

When he meditated and concentrated long enough he could almost remember Marengo. In those days he had been the one who had been in command, and now when he was tempted to be afraid he thought, "What would Napoleon have done?" And he knew that Napoleon would have been

contemptuous of the groundless fears which had so
terrorized the early life of Bunker Bean.

## Hidden Powers

*One historian had said that Napoleon 'won his battles in
his tent.' That was good enough for Bunker Bean. He would
also plan and organize and think the problem out before it
came to trial, just as Napoleon had done. Like Napoleon he
would see to it that nothing was left to chance. Napoleon had
permitted no exceptions to success.* Bunker Bean had a colored picture of Napoleon sitting on his great white horse on
an eminence overlooking a crucial battle which he was di-
recting with masterly waves of his sabre. Bunker Bean thrilled at the thought that this same great power still lay hidden
within his own breast, just waiting for expression.

*This mental stimulation proved a powerful tonic for the
ailing ego of Bunker Bean. He sat up all night to read the book
entitled The Hundred Days, which described Napoleon's battles.* True, it told of defeat, but also of how gloriously his
former self had taken it; of his escape from Elba, his return to
France, the march on Paris, conquering by the sheer magnetism of his personality wherever he passed. Bunker Bean's spirit bounded as he read of the frightened exit of the
enemy of Napoleon, that puny usurper who went down in
defeat before the mere rumor of Napoleon's approach. Then
he had been magnificent. He had been willing to stake everything on his own judgment and skill. But finally there
had come Waterloo and deathless ignominy. He heard again
the choked sobs of 'the old guard' as they bade their emperor
farewell. He felt the despairing clasp of their hands as those
strong bonds were finally severed that had held them together these many years.

Alone in his little room high above the glaring street
lights, the timid boy read *The Hundred Days* and thrilled to
a fancied memory of them. Now his breathing was stronger,
his blood ran faster in his veins as it went to nourish a body
that contained the essential portion of the great Bonaparte.
*Napoleon's contemporaries had called him an upstart, but the
historians had said that upstarts were men who believed in*

*themselves*. And Bunker Bean now believed with all his heart. As he read about himself, he forgot his mean surroundings and the timidities of spirit that had brought him thus far through life almost with the feelings of a fugitive.

## To Think Was To Act

Napoleon had exhibited his greatest powers as he led men to conquest. Inasmuch as there were now no wars to be fought, Bunker Bean must find some other outlet for his extraordinary abilities. He had been employed in a minor position in a business undertaking. *It seemed to him that this was the greatest field of adventure in which to employ his peculiar genius.* Bunker Bean knew that what he had once accomplished on the field of battle he would now repeat in the field of commerce. *He began to think about making money.* He knew nothing about the specific processes involved, but he felt sure that if he followed the principles that had been so productive in the past, he could not fail in the future.

The historians had said that Napoleon "had known human nature like a book." Therefore, he resolved to study human nature. One historian had said that *"with Napoleon, to think was to act,"* also that Napoleon was *"merciless in driving himself."* Therefore Bunker Bean would do again all of these things which had previously laid the world at his feet.

He had been working for small pay, but as he began to think about and develop these Napoleonic qualities of initiative and courage, amazing things began to happen. He was soon a different person. And other people began to notice the changes that were taking place in him. As a consequence, he was given more important work assignments, his pay was increased, and he began to advance with great rapidity up the positive incline of his success cycle. Now he knew that his friend had told him the truth.

## Before Napoleon Who?

Then he was struck by another thought. He knew that

for a short period of 52 years, he had been Napoleon. But certainly he should have some information about himself over a longer period. Who was he before he had been Napoleon? With these questions he again confronted his friend, and now that prosperity and money were coming his way, he could pay the medium well for whatever additional information could be obtained.

And he was not disappointed, because after the money had been paid, he learned to his further astonishment and delight that before he had been Napoleon he had been the greatest of the Egyptian Pharoahs. He had had a long and wonderful reign and had died at the age of 82 years. His death was deeply mourned by all of his people. He, Rameses, had been a ruler of great strength and character. He had been stern at times, but always just. His remains received the burial customary in those times, and his body was even now interred in the royal sepulchre, covered by the sands of the centuries.

As the Pharoah, he had been tall and handsome. He was so impressed with the account of the magnificence of the physical bearing of the Pharoah that he immediately employed the best tailor and had his clothing cut in such a way *as to give him the appearance of perfect physical development.* The effect produced so improved his form that he unconsciously strove to develop the appearance that the garment gave him. He expanded his chest, drew in his waist and stood erect. *"In beggar's rags most men are beggars; in kingly robes all men can be kings."* He felt he must achieve that kingly behavior that is said to distinguish royalty.

He Did Not Question

He had been thrilled by his deliberate acts of courage because they stiffened his spine. Now he would add to them royalty and grace and mental power. *He understood that such a marked advance in his spirit could not all be made in a day.* Such progress could only come after *long dwelling* in *thought and practice upon the qualities that were responsible for his splendid past.* He was a king and he must do what kings did. Kings were rich; therefore he would be rich. No sooner would his kingship be proclaimed than money would be in his hands. Money would come to him now as it had previously come to him on the banks of the Nile centuries before. He did not question *how* or *when – he only knew that it would come.*

No longer would he play the coward before trivial adversaries. He would direct large affairs; he would think big and he would live big. *Never again would he be afraid of death, or life, or policemen, or the mockery of his fellows.* Under this mental discipline his spirit grew tall and its fiber toughened. He knew that he was a king and others could not help knowing it also.

He sometimes thought about his present employer, and it occurred to him that had his employer lived with him back in Egypt he would probably have been a royal steward, a keeper of the royal granaries perhaps, or a dependable accountant. But he never could have risen very high because his 'lameness of manner was an incurable defect of the soul.' He pitied his employer for his weakness. Though his employer was successful and well-to-do, Bunker Bean was in a different class. He was a king. *But money and power came not only to kings, but to the kingly. Bunker Bean had been born to riches; he had been born a king, and would also do the things that characterized greatness.*

*Strength seemed to flow into him from his mental image of the strong, calm demeanor of the Pharoah.* When reliving his previous experiences he could believe no weakness of himself. He had once ruled a mightly people in Egypt. But also centuries later he had been Napoleon and had made Europe tremble under the tread of his victorious armies. He had made some mistakes in those earlier appearances. These he would not make again. *Bunker Bean believed himself to be both a wise king and a courageous soldier.* He thought courage at night and he awoke in the morning with a giant's strength. His thoughts were like a great inpouring of phosphorus into his personality. This gave him an iron will.

A Momentous Discovery

Then one day Bunker Bean made a tragic discovery. The medium was a fake. None of these important things that he had believed were true. He had been cheated for the sake of his money. Then he realized that he was not a king, that he was only weak, timid Bunker Bean, mean and insignificant. What a tremendous let-down! What an occasion for dejection and discouragement!

But in the years that Bunker Bean had believed himself a king, he had formed *the habits that go with success, and habits are not easily broken. It was now natural for him to do the things that great men did.*

And then Bunker Bean made another great discovery, and this time he was not deceived. He learned that great spiritual philosophy that, 'As a man thinketh in his heart, so is he.' And so it had been.

When he had believed himself to be a king, he had been a king. When he had believed himself weak, he had been weak. Had he not discovered the deception and gone on believing in himself, all would have been as before. Then he learned this great truth, that *"believing is all that matters."*

A new, molten, luminous, inspiring truth now ran through the mind of Bunker Bean. During these years no one had known that he had believed himself to be Rameses and Napoleon except himself and his former friend. But Bunker Bean had become wealthy while he had lived this myth of imagining himself to be great. He had gained wealth, power and prestige by believing in himself. Rameses and Napoleon had been only a crude bit of scaffolding on which he had climbed to success.

But the confidence that he had developed in himself could now endure without the help of the scaffolding. He would still think big and live big and be big. In spite of the discovery, his faith would still continue. The Corsican's magnetism would still prevail, and he, Bunker Bean, the lowly, would still have the power to magnetize, to thrill, to lead, and to accomplish. He would still remember that money, power, success and leadership came not only to kings, but to the kingly. The world would always be at his feet *"if he could only believe."*

Later he visited the tomb of Napoleon to pay his tribute to *the man who never lost faith in himself*. Even in those last sad days on the prison rock of his lonely island, his spirit had remained unbroken. How greatly Bunker Bean had profited from that courage and faith. He had developed a certain grim sureness of himself which would survive.

Emotion surged into the eyes of Bunker Bean, threatening to overwhelm him as he contemplated the great truths that "every man is born a king." "Every man is born to riches." "To believe is all that matters."

# Plans and Goals

# How You Can Duplicate
# The Success of Bunker Bean

*A Note from the Publisher –*
*The National Institute of Financial Planning, Inc.*
*Mark O. Haroldsen, President*

Bunker Bean reached great heights of success because he first truly believed in himself (even though he was tricked into doing so) and his own abilities. And second, because he followed an excellent game plan — a game plan that proved to be fantastically successful for Napoleon in war time and worked just as well when adapted to business during peace time.

This well-designed and carefully drawn road map for success combined with Bunker Bean's unwavering self-belief catapulted him to the very pinnacle of success. Stop and think how frustrated Bunker Bean would have become if, after learning who he was in his former life, he were unable to find any information about Napoleon (his former self), what he did, and exactly how he did it.

The frustrations that this would have caused would have completely killed his excitement and determination to lift himself up and become a truly successful person. Belief in one's self is most important, but that's only half the battle. Without a well-defined road map for financial success, or success in any endeavor, most people fail.

Have you ever read a very inspiring and uplifting book that got you all excited about your tremendous potential and then found that you slowly (or quickly in some cases) lost that excitement because you didn't have a specific task in which to direct your energies? You were frustrated because you lacked a plan that you could put into action immediately to harness your enthusiasm.

You see, knowing and understanding the different laws of success is one thing — applying them consistently into a workable game plan is another. Most people seem to have a difficult time in bridging that gap.

The average person can usually understand the general principles of success, but has a difficult time when it comes to putting them into action. What laws should be used, when and where, and how often?

## A Financial Success Bridge For You

An extremely well-constructed success bridge has been already built to fill this huge gap that slows or stops most people. You just need to develop enough determination to cross it. It is more than concepts — it is a bridge that I think you will find fills in all the blanks and will propel you to your own financial success. It will not only help carry you across the troubled waters to financial success, but will help you achieve success in all your activities and endeavors, and will help your life become a useful, fulfilling and enjoyable experience.

This complete guide to your financial and personal development is called The International Journal of Success.

There are many people who have built great fortunes by following the laws of success but have failed to develop themselves along the way. Such a person is only a 59 percent success. To be 100 percent successful you *must* succeed in the task of making the most of yourself so you are a contributor through your financial influence to the good of mankind and in making a better world. Because you have developed your potential, people will respect you as a person of stature and greatness.

## Get Started Now

Total financial freedom as a goal combined with personal perfection might seem utterly impossible to reach, but remember that there are many levels of achievement. Answer this question, "Are you really in a bad position if you shoot for the stars and only hit the moon?" The important thing is that you get started and get started now. Isn't the goal worth the effort? Probably the biggest effort is just getting started.

A good friend of mine told me of an employee that came to him saying, "I really want to quit and go out and get my law degree, but I don't know if it is the right thing to do. I'm 44 years old now, and if I quit working and go back to school, it will take five years to get my law degree and when I graduate from law school I will be 49 years old." My very wise friend helped make the man's decision by asking this question. "How old will you be 5 years from now if you don't go to law school?" The man now has a law degree and a thriving law practice.

Isn't it interesting that it's not really the large or extremely difficult obstacles that stop our progress to greatness and wealth or any other pursuit, but it is usually lethargy, sloth, laziness or simple inaction — *The things that we don't do stop us dead in our tracks.*

Sure I am trying to convince you to purchase **The International Journal of Success**, because it will financially better the position of the National Institute of Financial Planning; but just as importantly, I know that it will benefit you (if you apply it) more than you can imagine.

I know this to be true, because I have applied the principles and the game plan from this publication and have observed many, many others applying these principles with tremendous success.

## A Super-Producer

Sterling W. Sill, the author of "How to Personally Profit

from the Laws of Success" and the author of The International Journal of Success, has done much more than just *preach* these principles. He has obtained high success in virtually every field he has been involved in. Through the application of the principles and laws he believes in, Mr. Sill rose to the top of the New York Life Insurance Company and set performance standards of the entire company. He has spoken to literally thousands of audiences and is highly regarded as a public speaker. He has written 23 books and generated and been voice for a weekly radio program for 17 years.

Sterling W. Sill has amassed great personal wealth and is revered by his associates as a man of integrity and a super-producer with a keen ability to motivate others to achieve greater personal and financial success. Mr. Sill will do the same for you in The International Journal of Success.

Sterling Sill will inspire you to change and move in new directions. He'll share with you specific methods and material you can use to build yourself personally and financially.

I have listed below just a few of the topics and areas that The International Journal of Success covers:

- How other successful people have begun and how they have succeeded
- How successful people have applied the laws of success.
- Sterling Sill's Kash formula — What it is, how it works, and how you can apply it
- How to develop your own ideas and turn them into income.
- How to handle any competition.
- How to improve your own personality.
- How to develop leadership and initiative
- Developing your own great powers of: ambition, self-reliance, imperturbability, and industry.
- How to overcome fear (many adults will say they don't have fears now — only kids have fears — but some probing will expose dozens of deep-seated fears which cut into one's potential for financial success and successful living.)

- The knack of successful salesmanship (most people don't see themselves as a salesman; but successful selling (or persuading) of yourself, your ideas, your dreams or various products, etc., has always been the most important ingredient to a super-successful person.

## You Bet, I'm Trying To Motivate You

I have obviously been doing all that I possibly can to motivate you to buy this beautifully bound volume. I have done the same thing for my close friends and relatives. Why? Because, I know that The International Journal of Success can show you how to achieve absolute control of your personal and financial future.

## Small Price To Pay For Success

The cost is $42.00. These forty-two dollars may be the best investment you ever made, because if you will apply even part of Sterling W. Sill's success approach to your own life, the rewards, both personal and financial, will be fantastic! You'll finally understand specifically how financial independence can be obtained. But also you'll realize how this is a meaningless accomplishment unless you become a meaningful person at the same time. *Mr. Sill will teach you how to achieve both!*

## Make Your Decision Today

Make an investment in yourself and send for The International Journal of Success today.

Three easy ways to order:

1.) Fill in the coupon below and mail with a check or money order payable to The National Institute of Financial Planning, Inc., Dept. SWS-10,2612 W. 1030 So., Salt Lake City, Utah 84119.

2.) Fill in the coupon including credit card number,

signature, and expiration date of your card.

3.) Call **Direct** (long-distance) at 1-801-973-4053 and order by credit card.

### The International Journal Of Success
by
Sterling W. Sill
$42.00 (including postage and handling)

☐ Check or money
    order enclosed

☐ VISA

☐ Master Charge

Mail to:
National Institute of
    Financial Planning
Market Place Park
Dept. SWS-10
2612 W. 1030 So.
Salt Lake City, Utah 84119
Phone 1-801-973-4053

_____

(Name)

_____

(Address)

_____

(City)

_____

(State)                        (Zip Code)

Credit card no.:_____Expiration date_____
For credit cards, sign here:

_____

# 3
# The Law of
# OBJECTIVES

One law of success says that we must first have an objective. Before we set out on any journey, we ought to know something about where we want to go, how we are going to get there, and when we expect to arrive. With a tightly held objective, clearly visualized and greatly desired, success becomes easier.

For example, until the year 1926, no woman had ever swum the English Channel. Then an automobile company offered a red Buick convertible automobile and $2,500 in cash to the first woman who would accomplish this feat. A nineteen-year-old American girl named Gertrude Ederle wanted that automobile, so she decided to swim the English Channel in order to get it. Part way across, her strength began to give out, and she felt she couldn't swim one more stroke. But as she lay there waiting to be taken out of the water, she closed her eyes and before her imagination passed this red Buick convertible. This firing of her imagination gave her a new surge of strength, and she didn't stop again until she felt under her feet the sands of the opposite shore. This visualization of the objective made her the first woman to swim the English Channel, and without this tightly held objective, success would have been impossible.

In view of the magic motive power within ourselves, it seems unbelievable that many people should spend their lives trying to be successful and yet not have definite, well-defined, clear-cut daily, weekly, and monthly goals. This should be accompanied by a written record against which their daily performance may be measured.

The Roman emperor Maxim beheld in a dream a young maiden so beautiful that upon awakening he declared that he could not live without her. For years his envoys scouted the world in search of her. He knew what he wanted and had the determination to attain his objective, and so all his efforts were bent in that direction until it was accomplished.

So it is with each of us. We need an objective. We need something to tie to. We need a clear-cut ideal. We need a star to steer by. It has been said that "genius is the power to visualize the objective," and in order to visualize the objective, we must get it clearly and definitely in mind. We must have a focal point toward which we may work with all our might. If one is continually changing his objective, there can be very little progress. For the person who does not know where he is going, no winds are favorable, and if he has no time table in mind, his arrival may be both indefinite and uncertain.

Take a small electric magnet and see how it loses its strength as the distance is increased from the thing to be attracted. That is also true with our objectives. Unless we give it some special treatment, an objective beyond the reach of our present needs seems to us to be unimportant. This is a dangerous illusion if we are without the ability to compensate for this deception. Many people would trade their mansion in heaven for the smallest convenience in the present.

We can overcome any handicap placed upon us by learning to "prelive" the objective. That is, we should first get an objective; second, make it as definite as possible by writing out exactly what we want to accomplish weekly, monthly, and annually, as well as figuring out where we want to be forty years from now; and third, let our minds run ahead and live the last end first.

We may begin by cataloging in our imagination all the pleasures of our future objectives. Think of the advantages we may obtain for ourselves by not allowing ourselves to become discouraged. Think how happy and proud our spouses and children are of us. Think of the honors we will have from our company and the great regard in which we will be held in the community. Success is pleasant when it comes after a life of accomplishment and achievement, so we should magnify the importance and pleasure of each future accomplishment.

Albert E. N. Gray says that successful people are influenced most by the desire for pleasing methods. Loafing, going to the movies, and sleeping late may all be pleasant methods, but the result of having no money is unpleasant. Doing those things that failures don't want to do may seem to have some disadvantages, but the resulting success is very pleasant. If the end or objective is to be pleasant, then the method must include planning, industry, enthusiasm, will power, and determination.

One of the great differences between success and failure is that *the successful person focuses on the objective, whereas the unsuccessful person focuses on the present and sees nothing of great importance in the future.* The unsuccessful person sees only obstacles in his opportunities, while the successful ones sees opportunities in his obstacles.

The temporary upsets of the present can't hurt us much if our attention is fixed on the distant objective. For example, suppose that you have a long, hard tramp through the snow on a cold, stormy night. If you labor with no idea of the end and think only of the present cold, you are unhappy; but if you visualize the end and know that at the end of the journey there is a hot dinner, dry clothing, a warm fire, congenial friends, and a rich reward for your effort, that is an entirely different matter. The mental image of future warmth tends to overcome the present cold. To concentrate your thoughts on the dinner and the reward is far better psychology and good sense than to spend your strength thinking about how cold and disagreeable the weather is.

All of the joys and appetites are located in the imagination. If we keep our imagination focused on the objective, we have power. If we concentrate on the obstacle, we have discouragement. In one case we have motive and ambition; in the other, despair.

Napoleon once said, *"I see only the objective. The obstacle must give way."* Napoleon won his battles in his head before he won them on the field. He saw only the objective, and everything else was nothing. In the plentitude of his resources, every obstacle seemed to vanish. "There shall be no Alps," he said, and he built roads that climbed by gradation along the steepest precipices until Italy was within easy reach. Again and again he said to his men, "Beyond the Alps lies Italy," and in their minds they prelived all the delights they believed were in store for them at the end of the journey.

What a force was coiled up in the skull of Napoleon! He knew his business. He asked counsel of no one. He never blundered into success. He believed in Napoleon. His favorite rhetoric lay in his allusion to his star, and he styled himself the child of destiny. He risked everything; he spared nothing — neither ammunition nor money nor troops nor generals nor himself. That is the power created by a great imagination focused on its destiny. Napoleon was not a *good* man, but he had a powerful personality with immense capacities for sustained concentration. Someone called him "Organized Victory." He focused and pointed his life. He achieved centrality in his purpose. Psychologically speaking, he was all in one piece. Certainly before he started any undertaking, he knew where he was going.

We ought to practice regularly this kind of one-directional concentration with a clear-cut objective. This law of the objective has so many applications. We meet it in almost every act of life.

Some time ago, I attended a funeral at which, just before the funeral service and while the heirs were all present, the will of the deceased man was read. He had not visualized this hour when he wrote his will; when he wrote it, he was thinking of the present, not the hour preceding his funeral.

He did not foresee that when his will was read he would not be there to explain and make adjustments. Had his imagination run ahead and lived this funeral hour before he wrote the will, he might have saved a lot of heartbreak, and the attitude of his family at the funeral would have been much more kindly toward him and themselves. I learned then that a person can have a public relations problem even after his death.

The imagination is a pretty handy apparatus. We need to let it run ahead and get the spirit and the lay of the land of the future and then come back and report before we make our plans. We shouldn't trust our perspective, because unaided it will deceive us by subtracting importance from the future. This deception of perspective made Esau think that a mess of pottage today was more important than the birthright of the future.

We need to learn the art of living with our objective so that we can understand it before the time of our actual arrival; to make it as enticing as possible; to light it up so that it stands out like a great beacon. When we turn our thoughts to an objective, we raise up its image in our fancy, so we need to make that image of heroic size.

Gradually in our minds we can build our objective magnet stronger and stronger until success is easy and, like Gertrude Ederle, we may accomplish objectives that never before have been considered possible.

# Plans and Goals

# 4
# The Law of
# STRENGTH

The strength of man is found in the great creation of his mind. This power can become so great that sometimes when men harbor a great thought, they are to an extent taken captive by it. The idea possesses them and infuses them with its strength.

William James, the great Harvard psychologist, announced his program for getting this possession in his famous "as if" principle when he said, "If you wish to possess a qualification or an emotion, act 'as if' you already had it." Let it get hold of you. If you would be courageous, act "as if" you were already courageous. Shakespeare said, "Assume a virtue if you have it not."

The mind might also be compared to a great field where we grow and cultivate useful plants by design. Or we may bring forth a whole group of negative, destructive plants by default. Some people do not know that they must destroy even the undesirable seed in their minds or it will grow up to their ruin.

## It Is Thought That Counts

Every thought we think has an impact upon our personality and ultimate success or failure. And when we add to this force by expressing the thoughts in words, a double result is produced. It has never been determined how far the mind can go in changing one's character. We are certain it can make us insane. Or on the other hand, it can make us strong and successful. We can make ourselves sick, hungry, angry, happy, weak, or strong by self-suggestion. "There is nothing either good or bad but thinking makes it so."

> For as we think, so will we do.
> Guard well the portals of the mind;
> Let no discouragement seep through,
> Let doubt no lodgment find.
>
> More than's been done can still be done,
> Think this, and thinking then believe;
> So may the greatest goal be won
> Go on, think right, work hard, achieve.

Ruskin said, "A child went forth and became what he saw." Solomon said, "As a man thinketh in his heart, so is he." (Prov 23:7.) The law of strength says we are what we believe and feel. Certainly we are what we do.

Recently the British Army tested three men to determine the value of mental attitude on their performance ability. The strength of each of these three men was measured by a simple gripping device operated with one hand. They were found normally to have an average grip of one hundred pounds.

Then a scientist put them under hypnosis and made them believe they were very weak. Their utmost effort then registered only thirty-nine pounds. Keeping them under hypnosis, the scientist told them they were very strong. Their average grip rose to 142 pounds. When they believed in themselves, these men were nearly three hundred percent stronger than when they believed themselves weak. You can see the point and significance of this experiment.

*It is of far less consequence what others think of us than what we think of ourselves.* The pronouncement that "as a man thinketh in his heart so is he," has never been modified. We should never say depreciating things about ourselves out of a false sense of modesty or for any other reason. This recording device cannot tell when we are in earnest. The power of suggestion is tremendous, and well-intended, depreciating remarks added one on to the other are often very deadly.

If you want to develop courage, act like you already have courage. Don't keep telling yourself you are afraid. Don't tell yourself you are lazy. Don't even think you are lazy. Don't *be* lazy. To be possessed by strength, we should cultivate and think and act the things we would like to be. There is no dream that may not come true, wrote Arthur Simons. If we have the energy which makes or chooses our own fate, we can always in this world get what we want, if we will it intensely and persistently enough.

*So few people succeed because so few can conceive a great end and work toward it without deviating and without tiring.* But we all know that the man who works for money day and night with the right kinds of attitude and industry usually gets rich. The man who works day and night for spiritual or mental power gets that power. It is only the dreams of those light sleepers who "dream faintly" that do not come true.

Your Attitude About You

It is perfectly natural that things should not always go to our liking. But when one's attitude breaks down and he loses courage and develops a whining, complaining, belittling attitude, there is not much hope. The greatest ocean cannot sink the smallest ship until some of the water gets inside.

Never depreciate yourself. It is too dangerous. The man who makes promises lightly and then says, "I don't keep my word," is tampering with a great power. It is as though he is poisoning his own drinking water. *Don't be a promise breaker.* Don't get into the habit of dealing lightly with your word. After all, it's about all you have. Don't set a goal without doing your very utmost to redeem it. Don't give your word unless you are prepared to follow through. When these negative, weak, lazy attitudes get into our insides, we are in trouble. When the core starts to deteriorate, we are lost, but as long as we remain solid and vigorous at the heart, we are safe.

This attitude may appear to be a small thing, but how important it becomes if we work at it and make decisions and form habits around it. Anyone can think and act and be courageous for one day. But today's strength will help to make accomplishment easier for tomorrow. There is nothing inherent in being a sheep today that will help us to be a lion tomorrow. Suicide isn't always committed with the muscles of the arm. Failure is always suicide. Self-depreciation and negative self-suggestions are more destructive than poison or guns or razors or dynamite.

We know what a powerful effect the opinions of others have upon us. A slighting remark can sometimes change our life's course if we make ourselves susceptible to it, but how much more dangerous, though less obvious, when there is a consistent depreciating poison generating inside of us.

## Now Is The Time

The best road to success is to think big and act big and give substance to your greatest thoughts by putting them into action. Man's business is to work, to surmount difficulties, to endure hardships, to solve problems, to overcome the inertia of his own life. Keep in your heart a shrine to the ideal and upon this altar let the fires never die. We should immediately discard all of our philosophies of failure. We should throw out the weaknesses of evasion and procrastination. We should "meet the bull in the lane." We should adopt the philosophy of Henley, "I am the master of my fate; I am the captain of my soul." "Fear is with the faithless and faith is with the fearless."

The great Roman, Marcellus, taught his soldiers that it was base and ignominious to return from battle safe but unsuccessful. He had developed the vigor to wield the sword as well as to wear the crown.

Strength and weakness are both "inside jobs." Poison on the outside may not matter; poison on the inside is disastrous. Exercise makes us strong. We can start with little things that we can handle easily and increase our load at easy intervals and get into the success habit by being willing to pay the price. And this day by day exercise with the philosophy of strength and courage will make us grow strong and capable. Now is the time of our greatest opportunity. Seize it and teach it to obey. Shakespeare said:

> There is a tide in the affairs of men, which taken at its flood leads on to fortune; omitted, all the voyages of our lives are bound in shallows and in miseries.

> On such a full sea are we now afloat and we must take the current when it serves, or lose our ventures.

When we immerse ourselves in positive thinking and constructive attitudes, we saturate ourselves with success and then are possessed by it. This is the law of strength.

# Plans and Goals

# 5
# The Law of
# COURAGE

Each of us has two personalities: the personality we were born with and the personality we acquire after birth. It is our "acquired" personality with which we meet our daily problems. Certainly if we had only the personality with which we were born we would never get very far in any area of our lives. One of the most important qualities we can develop in our personalities is courage.

The dictionary says that "courage is that quality of mind which meets danger or opposition with firmness." It may be that we think of courage as being exhibited mostly on the battlefield or in some similarly spectacular place. However, in battle, one is usually fighting for his life; he is functioning under orders and some measure of compulsion, conditions in which it is difficult not to be courageous. But what about our courage when we are alone; when it is just as easy to retreat as it is to go forward; when we know no one will notice us and there will be no condemnation? This is probably the time, more than any other, when real courage is manifest.

## The Courage of Daily Life

We need a great deal of courage to hold us firm against the ordinary pressures of daily life. Just think how much talent is lost to the world for want of enough courage to enforce our daily convictions, or to back up our own planning. Every day sends to their graves obscure men whom timidity prevented from making a first start and who, if they could have been induced to try, might have gone a long way in the race for success. Our greatest fear should not be that our lives will someday come to an end, but rather that they may never have a beginning.

The primary test of courage is in the little things. Single great occasions do not make heroes or cowards; they simply unveil them to the eyes of others. Silently and imperceptibly we grow stronger or weaker until some crisis shows us what we have become. The house built on the sand may be just as secure as the one on the rock if there isn't any storm. It's trouble that reveals strength.

Everyone believes in planning, but how frequently we do not have the courage to follow through. We allow some little thing to throw us off the track. When we allow our plans and determinations and enthusiasms to break down, our whole character and personality is adversely affected, and what great value is lost thereby! Shakespeare said:

The purest treasure mortal times attest...
Is a bold spirit in a loyal breast.

### Inspiration To Continue

Courage is not easy to develop. We often let go just when we are about to succeed. The great Roman general Cato committed suicide on the very eve of his triumph. Shakesheare tells of England's King John, who lived in the fifteenth century. While he was engaged in a series of bitter wars, the battle had gone against him and he had decided to quit fighting. As he was waiting to surrender, one of his subordinates saw him and said:

But wherefore do you droop? why look you sad?
Be great in act, as you have been in thought;
Let not the world see fear and sad distrust
Govern the motions of a kingly eye:

Be stirring as the time; be fire with fire;
Threaten the threatener, and outface the brow
Of bragging horror: so shall inferior eyes,
That borrow their behaviours from the great,
Grow great by your example and put on
The dauntless spirit of resolution.
Away, and glister like the god of war.
                                    – *King John,* Act V, sc.1


With the new courage and enthusiasm inspired by an inferior, the king put his helmet back on, remounted his horse, and won the battle for England.


How Courage Is Developed

It doesn't take much figuring to find out that if we can develop this quality in sufficient proportion, it will be worth thousands of dollars a year to us in income and much more in satisfaction, and peace of mind. How should we go about it? Everyone must solve this problem for himself, but the following suggestions might be helpful.

1. One of the best ways to develop courage is to practice being courageous every day. We can be courageous in little things at first. Courage is made up of a lot of elements, like conviction, enthusiasm, persistence, and a desire to win. If we can use courage in little things, we will soon start winning victories. Someone has said that the morale of an army always breaks down when the victories are spaced too far apart. A successful year is a year filled with successful days. However, if our days are one-half good and one-half bad, we are doing as much to break down the habit of courage as to build it up.

2. We should fill our minds with courage. Read about courage. Think about courage. Admire courage in others. There are stories of heroism and success that will give our minds a positive charge and slant our personalities in the direction of courage. The mind, like the dyer's hand, is colored by what it holds.

3. We are also pushed forward by seeing the opposite quality in other people. Shakespeare said of someone who had lost his courage, "Thy nerves are in their infancy again and have no vigor in them." Cowards are always unattractive, and the life of a coward is a very difficult one that no one wants to imitate. Julius Caesar said, "Cowards die many times before their deaths; the valiant never taste of death but once. Of all the wonders that I yet have heard, it seems to me most strange that men should fear; seeing that death, a necessary end, will come when it will come."

4. We can develop courage by getting an appreciation of the things that life calls on us to do. He is very fortunate whose life's work and religious activities require initiative, resourcefulness, and the ability and courage to stand on his own feet, to do his own thinking, and to carry out his own plans. Any one of us can be successful and courageous until sundown, and if we can do it for one day, we can do it for a week. We can soon develop the stick-to-it-iveness and determination to go through with our program to the end of the year, and soon these great qualities begin to stand out in our lives and people will know us for what we have become.

5. We should try to keep all doubts and negative thinking out of our minds. "Our doubts are traitors, and make us lose the good we oft might win, by fearing to attempt." (Shakespeare.) Our fears blind us. It is so easy to quit and to fall by the wayside because we take the easiest course.

## A Necessary Ingredient

We pity the unfortunate people who try to build a successful, winning personality but leave out courage. They often go through life with a fearful, whining, complaining, grumbling attitude of feeling sorry for themselves, without the stamina to stand up and change the situations that may not be to their liking. Everyone is born beneath a signboard that points to courage and says, as did the fiery cross, "By this sign conquer." Courage not only points to success; it leads to pleasantness as well. Every successful life needs challenge. We need hurdles to overcome. We need problems to solve.

A number of years ago, a young man whose great ambition was to learn to be a football player enrolled at the University of Michigan. The coach put the young man to skirmish against the varsity, but he noticed that every time the play came the player's way, he cringed and turned away. The coach finally decided that the player was a coward, and he sent him back to the fourth string and forgot about him. However, in spite of his demotion and humiliation, the young man didn't quit. He had come to Michigan to learn to play football and that's what he was determined to do, whether it killed him or not. So he stayed on the job and did the best he could. The coach began to hear occasionally about the player's determination and mounting courage, and it didn't take long before he was on the first string. History knows this player as Tom Harmon, all-American, probably one of the four greatest football players of all time. He wasn't cowardly; he was just immature.

It takes a little time to develop courage, but it is worth working for. If we succeed today, success will be a little easier tomorrow. We learn by doing.

# Plans and Goals

# 6
# The Law of
# CONCENTRATION

Edison was once asked how he accomplished so much. He said, "It is very simple. You and I each have eighteen hours a day in which we may do something. You spend that eighteen hours doing a number of different unrelated things. I spend it doing just one thing, and some of my work is bound to amount to something."

If you want to be outstanding in any field, there is one important rule to observe: "Concentrate." Get one thing in your mind and heart and bloodstream. Put side blinders on your eyes so you cannot see all the distractions and temptations along the way. Forget the sidelines, and then put all the steam you've got right on the piston head and drive with full power down the main track. Keep out of the mud puddles; stay on the rails. Keep off the detours and sidings and drive straight ahead without continual startings and stoppings. Keep your mind on what you are doing.

When a person concentrates all of his energies in one place, he may hope to succeed. If he divides his time and talent among several enterprises, his chances of success are much less. But should he allow sidelines, chores, hobbies, politics, philanthropy, love of art, and myriads of other distractions to creep into and dominate his waking hours so as to become a passion, his success doom is sealed. It's a different application of the old principle of military success, which says, "Divide and conquer." Armies are weak when they are divided, and so are individuals.

### The Sideshow Attractions

The doctor or lawyer or merchant or prizefighter who specializes is the one who invariably goes places. And yet, every day we see persons who cannot resist the lures of the sideshow attractions. They still incline to the thought of cheating this powerful law by having sidelines and outside interests, and by that process they divide their power and subtract greatly from their effectiveness.

Ralph Waldo Emerson wrote two essays on this subject. One is entitled "Power" and the other "Wealth." The main theme in each is concentration. He said, in effect, "Stop all miscellaneous activities. Do away with distractions, other duties, property cares, chores, errands, diverting talents, and flatteries — all are distractions which cause oscillations and make a good poise and a straight course impossible." Distractions always untune us for the main purpose of our lives. Emerson said, "The one prudence in life is concentration; the one evil is dissipation."

As a gardener gets good fruit by severe prunings, thereby forcing the sap into one or two vigorous limbs instead of allowing it to dwindle into a sheath of twigs, so anyone headed for some great accomplishment gets the best results by concentrating his effort in one place.

### Keeping An Eye Single

A child may be perfectly content with his plaything until he sees something that some other child has. The child usually wants everything he sees and drops one thing after another as new attractions are presented. We are very much like children. We want too many things and are not constant and faithful to any one thing. The Bible says, "No man can serve two masters." It doesn't just say that some can't; it says *no* man can. It just can't be done. You can't ride two horses in

the same race. The Good Book says, "Keep your eye single."
That means to keep just one thing in the focus of your vision.
"A double-minded man is unstable in all his ways."

The greatest Christain missionary said, "This one thing
I do." That's why he became the greatest Christian missionary. A great Supreme Court Justice, in trying to indicate
the value of concentration and how it had helped him a-
chieve such a high place in the legal world, said "The law is a
jealous mistress. It tolerates no competition. The law says to
its devotees, 'Thou shalt have no other gods before me.'
Success in any field says just about the same thing."

Singleness of purpose and an unwearied will give power
greater than dynamite. It's a natural principle. We didn't
invent the law and we can't do anything about it, but it is the
law. I know a capable lawyer who was complaining about the
small income from his law practice. He had inherited some
money, and so I asked him how he had invested it. He was
very proud of the fact that he earned two or three percent
above the regular interest rate; but he had become so interested in how to buy mortgages at a discount that he didn't
have time to learn how to be a successful lawyer. He was
trying to inflate some investment dollars, and as a result, he
had deflated his income until it had almost disappeared.

Or take two doctors of equal possibility. One puts his
brains in his business and his money in the bank, while the
other tries to play the stock market and care for his scattered
investments. He loses his practice while the stock market is
going up, and he loses his savings while the stock market is
going down. How would you like to have a serious brain
operation performed by a doctor who had just lost $10,000 in
the market?

Such outside investment cares always detract from success. "Where your treasure is, there will your heart be also."
(Matthew 6:21.) This is an irrevocable law, and if we're going
to succeed, we'd better have our hearts and our investments
and our efforts and our attention in our own business.

## A Jack Of All Trades

We have only so many hours in a day. If we're trying to do four things instead of one, we can do two hours work on each instead of eight hours on one. But we always have to stop when we change directions. This means the loss of the great power of momentum. It also means we've lost the force and power and enthusiasm that comes from concentration.

"Jack of all trades and master of none" describes a human weakness of adults as well as children. We tend to want everything we see. If we take a fire hose and force the water out through the nozzle, we get great power. If we divide it into a spray, it falls softly with no force. The amount of sunlight that falls on the back of our hands is just pleasantly warm; but if we concentrate it through a convex lens and focus it into a pinpoint of light, we can develop enough heat to start a forest fire.

It is really surprising how many capable men fail because they "scatter their shot." Some have sidelines. Others let numerous little cares destroy their success. I know of one potentially capable businessman who tends his own vegetable garden, milks a cow, takes care of his yard, does his own landscaping, paints the house when necessary, does the plumbing. He runs the errands, does the shopping, carries his shirts to the laundry, and sometimes washes them himself. When his wife needs to go someplace, he does the baby sitting. Each fall he puts on an apron and helps his wife bottle a winter's supply of fruit. He wipes the dishes and helps care for the children until he probably doesn't know whether he is male or female, businessman or handyman.

## Errand Boy Or Businessman?

This man thinks he is saving money, but actually he is wasting the most valuable thing in the world — the power of concentration, one-directional, wholehearted effort. He also neutralizes his mind. He thinks like an errand boy and a baby sitter, not like a businessman. His mind is so occupied by this multiplication of little cares that it cannot cope with the important problem of becoming a success. He has even given up the peace and privacy and quiet of his own home by building an apartment in the basement. When the plumbing gets out of order, his renter just calls him; then he takes off his businessman's attitudes and enthusiasms while he becomes a toilet fixer. All of this brings the inevitable result: *his wife teaches school to support him.*

This is an extreme case, but there are many people who are continually stumbling over a number of little diversions and spoiling their chances to succeed. They are always starting and stopping, always on the detours or sidelines, always trying to save a few dollars or earn a few in competition with the errand boy, the house painter, and the plumber. The bank president doesn't polish the brass or sweep the floor. If he did, he probably wouldn't be bank president very long. A businessman should learn to think like a businessman. His time is too important to compete with errand boys. He should not spoil a magnificent achievement by turning off the fire of his enthusiasm while he fixes the plumbing.

Publisher's Note: If you are really sincere about reaching the very highest level of success, then Sterling Sill's superbly written The International Journal of Success is an absolute necessity. This beautiful bound volume will motivate you, inspire you, and direct you specifically toward your goals. If you are the type of person who never gives up, you may eventually reach your objective. With the aid of Mr. Sill's material that journey can be made more quickly and with fewer pains. See page 23.

# Plans and Goals

# 7
# The Law of
# TOTAL COMMITMENT

Pompey the Great was ruler of the vast Roman Empire half a century before Christ His most important field general was Julius Caesar. Caesar had had some differences with Pompey, and was considering marching on the capital to take matters into his own hands. In forty nine B.C. Caesar came to the Rubicon, a small river in Northern Italy that served as his territorial boundary line. The Rubicon was called "the sacred and inviolable." It was the line across which no general was ever allowed to pass without special permission from the Senate. If Caesar crossed the Rubicon it would be with the idea of making the entire Roman Empire subject to his will.

That was a momentous decision. It would immediately precipitate a civil war and divide the world between Pompey and Caesar. Caesar knew what the consequences would be if he tried and failed. He knew that many lives would be lost, in any event. Surely he must have hesitated before arriving at so great a decision, for he knew there could be no hesitation after the decision was made. Caesar carefully considered every angle. He explored every possible alternative. Then he made up his mind. He would march on Rome.

### The Die Is Cast

One part of Caesar's power came because of his ability to analyze a situation; another part came because of *his habit of always finishing what he started*. He was now starting the biggest undertaking of his life, to strike down the very heart of the world. Caesar said, "The die is cast." That expression marked the point where deliberation ended and action began. There would be no turning back. Then Caesar threw himself into the waters of the Rubicon at the head of his legions and the whole history of the world was changed.

Since this important event 2,000 years ago, the phrase, "crossing the Rubicon," has been used to indicate some decisive action of great importance. In one way the action of Caesar might become a sort of pattern for us. Our first step is to know where we are going; then we should carefully weigh the arguments. Then we should make a decision and be willing to stake everything upon our judgment. Once the decision has been made, every contrary thought should be banished. No energy should then be wasted in doubts, fears or reconsiderations, and nothing should be left undone which would help to bring about the projected accomplishment.

### Everyone Has His Rubicon

Whether Caesar was right or wrong is not the point of this discussion. The point is that every one of us also has a Rubicon to cross, and we should learn what we can about making decisions both on a personal and a group basis, and then learn how to carry them through to accomplishment.

When a Roman soldier joined the legions of Caesar, he took a pledge to hold the life of Caesar dearer than all else. That was his Rubicon. What should be our attitude [when we set financial goals for ourselves? Why should our responsibility to ourselves be any less?] . . . Or why should our minds be less firmly made up? Or why should our service [to ourselves] be less devoted than those who paid their allegiance to Caesar?

We often decide something one way when we are at the top of our condition and then abandon our plans when the tide begins to ebb. It is so easy to get cold feet or weak knees when a challenging set of circumstances confronts us. We become "accidental men" by putting our success even in the most important things under the control of circumstances. We get safely across the Rubicon only to begin suffering from a "faint heart," and then a retreat to the rear is the next logical step.

There are very few things that so quickly separate the sheep from the goats or that divide failure from success as this quality of a firm determination in the right direction.

## Burn Your Ships

To improve the quality of our leadership, we should see to it that no day is allowed to come to its close while any personal conflicts or problems are still undecided. Again, we might get a pretty good idea from Caesar. When Caesar went to capture Britain, he first landed his men and then unloaded his supplies. Then in the night he sent out men and burned the ships in which they had come. Then death was the only Roman alternative to victory. Under such circumstances most men fight with a vigor that never knows defeat. Then men learn to depend upon their own strength. When we know that we are cut off from outside resources we fight with a vigor equal to the force of desperation. There are many advantages in "burning our ships." When we cut off our chances to retreat, we increase our chances to succeed. Then, like Caesar, once over the Rubicon, there is only one direction to go and that is forward.

Some men often make the mistake when they start on an important undertaking of purposely leaving open a way for retreat. Then if things get a little difficult, they can always change their minds and their program without embarrassment. It is not an aid to success to be able to turn back from any point along the way. No one can really accomplish his maximum until he is *definitely committed* to his task and his mind has closed all lines of retreat. Retreat or surrender should not be made so easy as to actually invite us.

## Don't Be a Rip Van Winkle

A determined person allows no exceptions to success. Exceptions tear down a success habit faster than victories can build it up. Too often we say, as did the drunken Rip Van Winkle in Jefferson's play, "I won't count this one." Rip got into his difficulty because he never really made up his mind.

Most of us, including Rip Van Winkle, know what ought to be done. It is comparatively very simple to write out the formula for almost any accomplishment. But we fail either because we haven't really made up our minds or because we allow too many exceptions. We should make a definite landing and then burn our ships.

A friend once told me of visiting a certain town the day after a cyclone had swept through it. Only the solid, substantial structures were left standing. The weak, rotten trees and the light, flimsy buildings had collapsed and gone down before the wind. It is about the way in all departments of life. The weakest are always the first to go. A business crisis weeds out the inefficient businessman. Sickness strikes hardest at those with the least resistance to disease. The cyclone of sin and failure first removes from the ranks of leadership the undecided, the unsure and the undetermined. Only the stalwart and vigorous withstand the storm.

## Resolute Mind
## and Persistent Purpose

God gave man dominion over all things, including himself. Then how pathetic to see him crumble like a rotten building before the storm of some problem or inconvenience. There are no other qualities that stand so near to genius as a resolute mind and a persistent purpose. These two have won many battles after all other qualities have surrendered. Great generals say that there is usually an indecisive period in every battle, an awful moment when the soldiers are about ready to give up. This is the supreme "psychological moment" on which everything depends. Then the courage and faith of the rank and file are ebbing, and the soldiers feel like running away. These moments come in every department of life. Then is the real test of leadership. Then is the time when the leader must make the supreme effort to turn the tide. Workers must be inspired if they are to be kept from breaking.

Such an event is told of in connection with the Civil War battle of the Shenandoah Valley in 1864. The Union troops were demoralized and scattered. A New York reporter, standing at that hour upon an eminence overlooking the valley watching the disorderly retreat, wrote: "I am watching the awful destruction of the Union." Then a man on a big white horse came racing down the valley at top speed. He was carrying a pennant with two stars; it was the pennant of the Union general, Phil Sheridan. As he came, he cried, "I am here! Turn about. We will win. We will save the Union."

## Sheridan Is Here

It is reported that the men threw their hats into the air and cried like babies. They embraced each other shouting, "Sheridan is here." The effect was magic. The troops re-formed. By nightfall they had recaptured the Shenandoah Valley. The courage and decisiveness of one man had turned the tide for thousands. Such is the power of great leadership. Such is your power.

The most hopeful moment in any life is when there comes into it the dawning of a fixed purpose with definite plans for accomplishment. Then we are able to say, "The die is cast," and we dive into our own Rubicon and with firm strokes head for our destination.

# Plans and Goals

# 8
# The Law of
# ADVANTAGE

One of the most important differences between modern men and those of earlier periods is in the fact that modern men have invented and learned to use tools to make their work more effective. For example, a person whose large automobile may have a flat tire couldn't begin to lift up the front end of the vehicle by himself to change the tire, so he gets out of the trunk of the car a little tool that he calls a jack. He puts it under the front of his car, turns the crank to the jack, and, with almost no effort or strain, quickly lifts the entire end of the automobile into the air.

If one were to put a 500-pound weight on one end of a rope and a 150-pound man on the other end and suspend them in the air with a rope through a pulley, the weight would drop to the ground and crash the man into the pulley. But if this same rope were run through a block and tackle and again suspended in the air with the man on the end of the rope and the 500-pound weight on the block and tackle, this time the weight could be lifted up and the man lowered. By means of a simple lever, a man can lift several times more weight than he otherwise could. We call this ability to multiply our strength by the use of tools "mechanical advantage."

### Tools Make Giants of Ordinary Men

By another device, a man with a pump and some water might lift a great battleship over a mountain by means of locks constructed for that purpose. The battleship is sailed into the lower locks and water pumped in until the locks are full. The locks are arranged like stairs, and when the lock is full, the gates on the stair above are opened and the battleship is floated in on the new and higher level; then the gates are closed behind it. When water is pumped up to the new level, the battleship is again lifted up, and the process is repeated.

Though the compartment in which the battleship floats may be only a hundred feet wide and the battleship ninety feet wide, the water can force the battleship up; and this simple process, if repeated enough times, could carry the battleship to the top of the mountain. Not only would it go up the mountain, but the same water, with almost no effort or pump, could be used to lower the battleship down the other side of the mountain. The jack and the block and tackle and the water and the lever may not have any power in themselves, but they can make giants out of ordinary men who learn to use them properly.

This law of advantage can be applied in other areas of our lives. For example, suppose a man buys a $10,000 family income insurance policy and pays a small monthly premium of less than $35. Right that instant, if he is accidentally killed, his family will receive $10,000 in cash, $100 a month for twenty years, and another $10,000 in cash at the end of the twenty-year period, or a total of $44,000. In one hour, the man could create an estate in the event of his accidental death that in the ordinary ways of accumulating interest and principle would require over forty years of making payments. Like carrying the battleship over the mountain, this estate can be created with only a small part of the effort that would be ordinarily required.

An automobile jack is a simple gadget with no power in itself, and yet, if we have automobile trouble, how handy it becomes. It's a very foolish man who starts across the desert without an automobile jack. Likewise, a life insurance policy is a simple financial tool, but when our physical breakdown comes, what a tremendous thing it is.

## Tools of Social Advantage

Similar to what we might call the laws of mechanical and financial advantage is what we might call the law of social advantage. For example, there's a little "jack" that we might carry with us that is called a sense of humor. Think how much less effort it is to jack up our social automobile if we have this tool than if we don't have it. There's a social "block and tackle" that we call a smile. An electric lineman once came in contact with a live wire, and the left side of his face was paralyzed. The jury, in considering the damages, asked him to smile, but he could only smile on one side of his face; they subsequently awarded him $100,000 damages. If half a smile is worth so much and yet it costs nothing at all, then we certainly ought to have it in our "social tool chest" and keep it in good working order, ready for constant use. It's worth a million dollars and yet it doesn't cost a cent. However, we should also remember that one who *doesn't* smile may not be any better off than one who *can't* smile.

There's a social "lever" that we call reputation. What multiplied power and greatly increased strength it gives us if we have earned the right to have people think of us as persons of unquestioned integrity who are fair under all circumstances, regardless of the consequences! A man of genuine character can carry a social battleship over a mountain with strength to spare.

## Multiply Your Personal Power

Men have developed extensions to the senses. Through the power of television, we may see across nations; with a telephone receiver, we may hear across continents, though oceans roll and roar between; with a microphone, our voices may be heard around the world; with the wings of jet propulsion, we can travel faster than sound. However, the greatest area for extending ourselves is through the use of the social, mental, spiritual, or personality tools that multiply and magnify our strength.

The Master gave us a formula for increasing our strength when he said, "If ye have faith as a grain of mustard seed, ye shall say unto this mountain, Remove hence to yonder place; and it shall remove; and nothing shall be impossible unto you." (Matthew 17:20.)

Prayer and dependability also multiply our personal power, and we ought to make a list of these marvelous instruments that come to us without cost so that we may store them in the "toolshed" of our lives and use these powerful laws of advantage to make giants of ourselves.

# Plans and Goals

# 9
# The Law of the
# BOOMERANG
## "The million-dollar philosophy that's absolutely free"

How would you like to possess great personal power? How would you like to be trusted and respected and loved? How would you like to have people always treat you exactly the way you would like to be treated? Here is some good news for you: you can actually have all of those things. The answer as to how you can get them is found where the answers for many of the other important questions of life are found — in the scriptures.

### The Golden Rule

Jesus was not just a great teacher — he was also a master of human relations. The greatest statement on public relations that was ever made is known as the Golden Rule, though this title is not found in the scriptures. The Master said, "Therefore all things whatsoever ye would that men should do to you, do ye even so to them." (Matthew 7:12.) This principle has possibilities of both good and bad. Someone has referred to it as the law of the boomerang, meaning that whatever we throw out, we receive in return. A cartoon recently appeared in a newspaper showing two natives from the bush country of Australia. One was saying to the other, "I would like to get me a new boomerang but I can't get rid of this one I already have."

This powerful instrument involving human emotion has also been called the law of retaliation. It involves the ancient philosophy of an eye for an eye and a tooth for a tooth, except the offense is always returned with compound interest. For example, the bombs are getting bigger and the national machines of war are becoming more powerful so that each nation can pay its enemies back with multiplied destruction. In its application to the individual, if we would like to have someone punch us on the nose, we don't need to *talk* to him about it or try to *bribe* him to do it. All we need to do is just give him a good healthy sock on the nose, and we'll be socked in return. We can depend on it. If we want someone to invite us to his house for dinner, we invite him first to our house to dinner and then he will see to it that we get a little better dinner at his house than he got at ours. If we want someone to like us, we must like him. If we want to be trusted, we must trust.

## Disregarded by Most

This law represents one of the most powerful combinations of words in the language. In substance it was taught many centuries before it was enunciated by Jesus in Palestine. It was proclaimed by Confucius, Zoroaster, and Mohammed. It has been effectively practiced by many successful statesmen, businessmen, authors, and other human beings. But while this is the greatest statement of public relations that has ever been written, the great bulk of mankind has actually never done very much about using it for their good.

We are like human magnets. Our deeds, our attitudes, and even our thoughts attract in kind. Like begets like. When we know in advance how people will react, great power is placed in our hands, if we have the courage to use it. When we thoroughly understand these laws of action and reaction, then we can stimulate any desired response in other people. If we want smiles, we must give smiles. If we want people to like us, all we have to do is like them. If we speak ill of someone behind his back, he retaliates in kind, only magnified.

## Returning Good for Evil

If we want to get the best of an enemy, we should be friendly to him. The hottest coals of fire ever heaped on the head of one who has wronged us are the coals of human kindness. To return good for evil is a method of attack that he does not understand; it leaves him baffled and powerless, and we can easily dominate him.

But think what happens when we try to force our way, when we go around with a chip on our shoulder, when we push people around and insist on our rights. We get back evil for evil, gossip for gossip, unfriendliness for unfriendliness, except it is multiplied.

Someone put this idea down in verse; he said:

Here lies the body of William Jay —
He died defending his right of way.
He was right, dead right, as he sped along,
But he is just as dead as if he'd been wrong.

## It Can Change Lives

When we have mastered the simple philosophy contained in the Golden Rule and have learned how to put it into practice, we will have learned much about public relations, salesmanship, teaching, and business success. We will also have mastered ourselves and will have learned how to cultivate self-control.

The Golden Rule is a great way of life. It controls a power that is too strong for anyone to resist. It conquers everything before it. If a person can learn how to use it, it can change the whole course of his life in thirty days. *It's worth a million dollars, and it is absolutely free.*

Try this formula for a few weeks and see what the result is. Above everything else stamp it into you hearts, put it in your bloodstream, and get it into your muscles. Remember the message of this great law: *"Whatsoever ye would that men should do to you, do ye even so to them."*

## Plans and Goals

# 10
# The Law of
# PROFESSIONAL PERFORMANCE

Demosthenes once made a great speech in which he said in part: "It is impossible, I say, to have a high and noble spirit while you are engaged in petty and mean employment. For whatever be the pursuits of men, their characters must be similar." One's occupation and his attitude toward it, largely make the man.

*That's a great idea for anyone working toward any accomplishment to remember.* Just think of men in the different lines of work, and you will see that what they do and how they do it impresses itself on what they are. There are some kinds of work that degrade. There are other kinds of work that uplift and ennoble, but the work itself may not differ as much as the way in which it is done. A great man once said, "It is not where you serve, but how you serve that is important." Some workmen can make the most petty work noble, while others make the most noble work mean.

## Guilt by Association

Here's another example of the old *law of the boomerang,* which says we get back that we throw out. It is sometimes a very disturbing fact that our chickens come home to roost. If you are associated with a disreputable company, or associated with fourth-rate people, others will say, "We cannot afford to trust this man's judgement in other matters." The kind of associates we have "mold us into their own image."

Shoddy work makes shoddy workmen. A great psychologist once said, "How would you like to create your own mind?" But isn't that exactly what everybody does? *The mind is made up of what it feeds upon.* The mind, like the dyer's hand, is colored by what it holds. If I hold in my hand a sponge full of purple dye, my hand becomes purple. If I hold in my mind and heart attitudes of great enthusiasm and faith, my whole personality is colored accordingly.

## Our Employment Colors Our Life

Isn't it interesting that we create our own success or failure by how we think and what we do. There are many kinds of work, ranging from the most noble to the most petty. Some people work with their hands, some with their minds, some with their hearts. Some work with personalities. Some work with things; some work with people.

But whatever our activity, our employment colors our life. Someone has tried to make a destinction between a business and a profession. In a profession, welfare comes first, money-making second. A profession is an occupation that involves a substantial education. It is mental rather than manual. A profession implies scholarship. This distinction may be a delicate one and hard to make with precision, but if our character and personality are to be molded and marked by our employment, we ought to make certain that our employment is of the highest order.

It is certainly possible for two people to be working at the same thing and one's work to be noble, the other profane. One is professional; the other degrading. Think of a good and bad lawyer or a good and bad teacher. We might write our own definition of a profession and then see to it that our performance corresponds.

## A Solid Foundation

It is an intriguing thought that we build our own minds and determine our own possibilities. We are a reflection of the kind and quality of the work we do. It's tragic to think how a human life, with the possibilities of great professional service, can be debauched and prostituted by shortsighted-ness, thoughtlessness, or a false self-interest. We need more than a smart sales talk to get us successfully through life. We need a sound philosophy of living. Men who develop this ancient sense of mission to perform are building their houses upon solid foundations.

In recent years there has been a tremendous increase in psychiatric problems. The cause of mental breakdown is usually associated with emotional life. Mental breakdowns are sometimes attributed to mental conflicts, lack of devotion to a cause, lack of worthy standards, or a sense of futile effort.

Psychiatrists say that many patients never learn to look inside themselves; they never learn to examine their way of living and thinking. The reason they do not is obvious: they are not going to see what they do not want to see. If they did, all of their defenses would be destroyed. As a consequence, men become bewildered, confused, and self-defeated by building their houses upon the sand. Shakespeare's Othello said, "I have lost the immortal part of myself, and what remains is bestial." That was so because of what he did. In varying degrees, this is a common experience.

## Be a "Professional"

Now suppose, therefore, that we think of our work from the point of view of a "profession" in the best meaning of that term. If there is anything in what we do that is in any degree destructive to the best interests of human beings, it should immediately be eliminated.

However, on the other hand, if we, like the dyer's hand, can be "colored" by the great principles of integrity and fairness, just think what great meaning our work will have for us. Our life's possibilities for service, scholarship, self-improvement, and devotion to a worthy cause is unlimited.

Cheap products make cheap men. Fortunately, nature has a way of eliminating from the system of society many of those who are unfit or unworthy to survive. But usually this is not done until after great harm has been done.

There are many people who would not only live longer but more successfully if they would lavish a little less affection upon themselves and their own comforts. It's an old story that he that loseth his life in his work shall find it.

Whatever be the acts of other men, each of us personally has the opportunity to make of his work and his life a profession in the highest sense of the term, and he may write his own definition.

It is impossible to have a high and noble spirit while engaged in petty and mean employment. Whatever be the pursuits of men, their characters must be similar. And our service, when conducted on the highest plane, builds a high and noble spirit which the great Demosthenes held to be one of the greatest of all accomplishments.

# Plans and Goals

# 11
# The Law of
# FEAR

A theory is held by some people that fear is a great curse sent to punish those who live upon this earth. Nothing could be farther from the truth, and those who adopt this philosophy are injured by it. Actually, the ability to fear was put into our personalities to strengthen our courage, protect us from harm, and increase our godliness and our capability for accomplishment.

As a consequence of this misunderstanding about the purpose of fear, many people try, to their own detriment, to avoid or distort or sidestep this important and constructive emotion and the natural fruits that would otherwise come from it. We ought to thoroughly understand the fact that far from being man's enemy, fear is a great and constructive force for good if one is afraid of the right things at the right time. The ancient Greeks even erected a temple so they might show proper reverence to the god of fear.

## Fear as a Motivator

Fear is the beginning of wisdom, the father of prudence, caution, and foresight. It is a stimulant that keeps us on our feet and moving. A child stays away from fire because of fear; men are encouraged to obey the law because of fear; a young person goes to school and works and prepares himself in life because he fears the results of ignorance and unemployment. We control our conduct because we fear a bad reputation. We work and save because we fear want. We plan and think because we fear the result of misdirected effort. So it naturally follows that we should stimulate rather than destroy our fears.

Fear is the warning flag that prompts us to stop, look, and listen. It makes us sharp and aggressive and keeps us on our toes. It puts us on our mettle. The world would indeed be a chaotic place without the great and valuable controlling emotion-fear. The squirrel would not store up his acorns if he were not afraid of the winter's cold and hunger. The lawyer would not prepare his court presentation so meticulously if he were not afraid of failure and defeat.

Fears of failure and weakness and consequence also tend to make a nation great and strong and safe. Sometimes in times of peace and ease, a potentially powerful nation may be idle and tend to become fat, lazy, and listless. We might recall when the enemy attacked Pearl Harbor and how America immediately sprang to its feet like a giant. Its muscles became taut; its attention came into focus; its brain became alert; its creative genius began to produce unheardof inventions and unbelievable miracles of mass production, all because it was angry and afraid.

Fear pours into the blood a powerful element that multiplies our strength. If our house catches fire, in our excitement we may be able to carry the piano outdoors to save it from the flames, but after the fear has subsided, it would take four people to carry it back in. We can run faster or fight harder or do more work or be more faithful when we are afraid.

Certainly we ought to be afraid of bigotry and pettiness and dishonesty. Fear is also nature's method of individual protection to keep us all safe, honest, and prosperous with a feeling of security for our entire lives.

## The Destructive Power of Fear

Fear as an element in education cannot be ignored. It is like a fire; it is a good slave but a poor master. Fear is like strychnine — a great stimulant, but if you take an overdose of either strychnine or fear, it usually signals the end. Let fear get out of control to a point where it becomes panic or hysteria and it causes great destruction.

Many people are always predicting unreasonable calamities, tending to stampede their own reason and the reason of other people. The road to duty and success is hampered by one's fears. Unreasonable fears make one blind and deaf and sometimes dumb, but if it is understood and controlled, fear can become our greatest ally. Shakespeare said, "To fear the worst, oft cures the worst."

## Fear as an Ally

Motivated by a substantial, well-controlled, well-understood fear, our spiritual and mental muscles can become strong. If we learn how to properly handle our fears, we become courageous, industrious, and productive.

We should not fear fear, but should recognize it and welcome it as an ally, sent to give us judgment and muscle and protection. In fact, the only place where it is possible to develop courage is in the presence of fear. Fear is the moving cause of most accomplishment. We should try not to avoid it, but rather to develop it, for if we would eliminate the cause, we must also do without the result. If fear is removed from the young man, it may mean the security will be taken away from the old man. We should only learn to recognize, appreciate, and control it.

It is a perversion of our personalities to let fear inspire timidity, paralysis, dread, dismay, hysteria, or panic. Shakespeare gave us one of our greatest philosophies when he said, "Cowards die a thousand times before their death; the brave man never tastes of death but once." He said, "Of all the wonders that I yet have seen, it seems to me most strange that man should fear, seeing that death, a necessary end, will come when it will come." We may not always be able to change the time of our death, but we can always be better prepared for it. After all, most of the things we fear are corrected before they happen. The most difficult memory test is to try to remember the things we worried about ten years ago.

> Of all our troubles great and small;
> The greatest are those
> That never happen at all.

And so we might say to ourselves, "Let not fear prevail above thy will." (Apollo.)

# Plans and Goals

# 12
# The Law of
# PERSUASION

One of the greatest instruments in civilization is the power of persuasion. The dictionary says that persuasion is to win over, by entreaty, reasoning, or by an appeal; to recommend for acceptance, to allure, convince, impel, induce, lead or move. To persuade is to bring the will of another to a desired decision by some influence short of compulsion. One must be convinced that the earth is round before he can be persuaded to travel around it. Persuasion is dependent upon conviction. It is commonly held to be the orator's first purpose to convince, in order that he may persuade. To coax is a slighter word than to persuade, seeking the same end by a shallower method.

## America: A Nation of Salesmen

The work of a politician, the minister, the salesman, and other leaders is made up of a large part of persuasion. Much of the advancement in the world comes because of persuasion. The bathtub or the horseless carriage, the iceless refrigerator, the locomotive, or the steamship were not accepted at first. They had to be sold. The difference between America and some other nations is that we are largely a nation of salesmen who persuade each other to better ways of doing things.

Some of the ingredients of persuasion are as follows:

1. *Clarity.* Be sure of your terms so that you will avail yourself of clear definitions and exact meanings. Then your listener will get exactly the right shading and meaning that you intended. Someone has said that there are no synonyms.

2. *Regard for whatever may be the subject of your persuasion.* It is also necessary to have regard for the person we wish to persuade. He must also feel kindly toward us if the best results are to be obtained.

3. *Understanding.* We must know the mind and heart of the one we would persuade. We must know what principles he acknowledges, what things he loves, and then observe in the thing in question what affinity it has with the acknowledged principles or with the objects in which he takes delight.

4. *Reasonable.* The proposition should be shown to be reasonable and right.

5. *Pleasure.* The art of persuasion consists as much in that of pleasing as in that of convincing, so much more are men governed by likes than by logic.

6. *Profit.* Persuasion is so much more simple when a person can be shown that the proposition is in his interests.

7. *Conviction.* We must be convinced before we can carry conviction to someone else. One must be a convert before one can be a salesman. Belief is all important in persuasion and must be felt by persuader and the persuaded.

8. *High standing of persuader.* It is much easier to persuade a person when he has confidence in you and holds you in high regard. Lincoln said, "If you would win a man to your cause, first convince him that you are his sincere friend." Your point of view is greatly changed when you like the man who is making the presentation. The conspirators who stabbed Caesar wanted Brutus on their side because, as Cassius said, "He sits high in all the people's hearts and that which

would appear amiss in us, his countenance like richest alchemy shall change to virtue and to nobleness." Shakespeare, etc.)

9. *Knowledge.* A salesman must know the product and how it will help his prospect to accomplish his objective.

10. *Enthusiasm.* Enthusiasm is one way we give to somebody else the conviction of the value of our reccommendation.

11. *Clear expression.* We must be able to effectively express our ideas so he will feel as we feel.

The power of Persuasion is the power to enlighten, to lead, to convince, to please, to produce action, to profit. The Power of Persuasion is one of the greatest powers ever placed in the hands of men.

# Plans and Goals

# 13
# The Law of
# IDLENESS

It's a natural law that out of idleness comes weakness. Nature hates idleness in all its forms. She gives continuous life only to those elements which are in use. Tie up an arm or any other part of the body in uselessness and the idle part will soon become lifeless. Reverse the order and give an arm more than normal use, such as the activity engaged in by the blacksmith who wields a heavy hammer all day long, and the arm grows strong.

This law governs physical, mental, spiritual, social, and personality development. It says that the way to growth is activity, whereas the way to death is idleness. Running water purifies itself, but the stagnant water of an inactive pond becomes impure and unhealthy, and so do the cells of a sluggish body or an inactive brain. Laziness is the influence of an inactive mind upon the cells of the body.

Nothing is more common than mental inertia. For every ten people who are physically lazy there are ten thousand with stagnant minds, and stagnant minds are breeding places of fear, ignorance, sin, and crime. The person who is active generates power and breeds courage. The one who has power in his righteousness has little to fear, while the un- profitable servant allows his fear to destroy his faith. We can build up our faith and our industry to where it will eliminate our fear.

### Earning Our Bread

One of nature's laws tells us that we should earn our bread before we eat it. When young people want too much ease at the beginning of their lives, they are usually doomed to failure. Rest comes only after it has been earned. When nature sees a young person engaged in inactivity, she assumes that he wishes to become a nobody and immediately begins granting his request.

Many otherwise capable people succumb to this negative law. Often the sons of wealthy families are not properly impressed with the necessity for effort. They try to slide from first base to home plate on their family name, and, in conformity with this law of ease, they lose their inheritance. When one sits too long on his cushions of advantage, he goes to sleep and is soon eliminated from the race.

There are others who fail because their first efforts miscarry, and they lose heart and quit. Success likes to be sought after and wooed. The Master himself said, "Pray without ceasing." Life does not always grant one's first petition. Obstacles are put in our way to strengthen us but when we misunderstand their purpose and allow them to breed discouragement — that is, when we cannot tell the difference between temporary setbacks and permanent failure — then we turn off our effort and succumb to the penalties of the law of idleness.

### Opposition Strengthens

Temporary failure is nature's great crucible in which she burns the dross from the human heart and so purifies the man that he can stand harder usage. It is said that fortune often disappoints him whom she secretly anoints. A poet has written:

How she hammers him and hurts him,
And with mightly blows converts him.

Hard hammering is always necessary to make the finest steel. Because of the law of opposition, it is necessary that people be acquainted with obstacles and rough going. Most men develop faster after they understand opposition, which arouses them to greater action. Our strength grows out of our weakness. Not until we are kicked and stunned and shot at is our indignation awakened. When he is punished and pushed, tormented and defeated, a person has a chance to learn something. And when we cease to look for a life of ease, we have a chance to go places.

Naturally we would all like to have someone give us detailed directions as to how to succeed and then give us the push that would carry us across the goal line. No one can succeed for us except ourselves, and no two persons find the same way to the goal. Each must find his way there by himself. Effort and struggle — both mental and physical — are the way by which we achieve. Life was never intended to be just a pleasure trip or a downhill ride. It is an uphill journey. It is a conquest, a long series of difficulties and obstacles to be mastered.

## Weariness is Not From Overwork

Don't worry about getting tired, for weariness usually does not come from overwork, but from lack of interest in what you are doing. The muscles never grow fast until we give them some heavy usage. The possession of potential power and the use of it are two different things. The use of our strength makes us powerful, while the pursuit of easy things makes us weak. It is seldom the work we do that makes us tired. Most likely are we tired because of the work we have left undone.

When things are really clicking for us, we seldom get tired, and we can then accomplish many times the work we previously did. Fatigue is caused not by work but by worry, frustration, and resentment. The kite always rises against the wind, not with it. The strongest oak tree of the forest is not the one that is protected from the storm and hidden from the sun, but the one that stands in the open where it is compelled to struggle for its existence against the winds and rains and scorching sun. A great oak struggling in the wind sends down a stronger root upon the windward side. In the same way, the Lord fits the human back to the burden. When we are struggling, we grow. When we retire so that we can take things easy, we are usually on our way out.

The law of success says that idleness always leads to deterioration and death, and these should be avoided by those who would be strong.

# Plans and Goals

# 14
# The Law of
# SELF-CONTROL

One of the most recent engineering marvels of our age is power steering, by the aid of which a 300-horsepower engine in a car of several thousand pounds traveling at tremendous speed may be controlled by the pressure of one finger. Engineering science, through brakes, steering devices, and other inventions, has given man fingertip control over the most powerful of engines.

If someone would like to gain everlasting fame, he could do it by perfecting a device whereby a man could get a comparable degree of control over himself.

### Different Degrees of Control

A man usually has great authority over his limbs. If he wills that his finger bend, it will obey. His legs move merely at the suggestion of his will. It's wonderful to contemplate mental power with authority over physical substances. This authority has different degrees of control. A man has rather complete control over his fingers but little or no control over his heart or liver. If he wills that his eyes close, they respond, but if he wills that his heart stop, it pays no attention. Between these two extremes lies all the rest of our self-control. One has great authority over his feet, not quite so much over his tongue, and, in diminishing order, his ideas, his industry, his feelings, his emotions, his instincts.

The dictionary says that to control is to exercise a directioning, restraining, or governing influence. Self-control would, therefore, mean to exercise direction, restraint, motivation, and government over our organs, our faculties, our emotions, and our personalities; and the ultimate in self-control would be to obtain a sort of fingertip power-steering arrangement so that all of our faculties and inclinations would respond to our slightest touch. Then our personalities or ideas would never run wild nor would our emotions get out of control.

We should not be too discouraged if this jurisdiction is not complete at first. All living things at their birth are small and misshapen. Even ideas are not usually born fully symmetrical, well-formed, with maximum power and polish. That is a matter of subsequent growth and development. One of the great purposes of training is to increase our authority over our component parts.

Try to think of anything in the world that would be more important than one little gadget that would spell self-control for us. It would include in it all of the following:

Self-inquiry
Self-analysis
Self-criticism
Self-correction
Self-knowledge
Self-instruction
Self-motivation
Self-improvement
Self-reliance
Self-control

## Mind Over Matter

*The greatest accomplishment is to train the mind to extend and increase its authority over the body.* The business of living is probably one of the best places to teach ourselves self-control. Life is also the place where we are most highly rewarded for the development of self-mastery.

One of the first steps toward self-control is planning. We know something about what we must do, and we also should understand our own resources and shortcomings. Then once every day we should sit down and plan and think and analyze and reason. This is where we make a program for the activities of the day, but it is also where we make decisions and build morale for ourselves and decide on our projected improvements and our goals. The work that one does above and beyond his objective is highly stimulating. It is helpful to the personality to feel that we are going beyond the expected, that we are making a superior effort.

## Success, Power, and Happiness From Self-Control

*Checkup and follow-up are important.* We should never give anyone an assignment and then fail to check up. It's even more dangerous with ourselves, for we should develop the very best ways to motivate, restrain, and guide ourselves.

In our work every day, we should watch and practice our control — time control, idea control, enthusiasm control, industry control, accomplishment control, and so forth. This is one way to become a great doctor or a great lawyer or a great salesman or a great human being. Self-control is the most effective means to any kind of success, power, and happiness.

# Plans and Goals

# 15
# The Law of
# HEALTH

An old wisecrack says, "I am not in business for my health." However, anyone who has thought about this very much knows that it is not an accurate statement.

The dictionary describes business as that activity which life says one has to do or should do. As soon as one is born, life begins to impose upon him some service or duty or mission that makes up the business of life. When Jesus was twelve years of age, he was aware of this fact, for he said, "Wist ye not that I must be about my Father's business?" (Luke 2:49.)

The business of living is broken up into several vocations or avocations, and whether we like it or not, we are soon confronted with the business of making a living. Everyone becomes a member of a family business — first as a child then as a husband or wife, then as a parent. Everyone also becomes involved in the business of keeping himself amused and happy. A Book of Mormon scripture says, "Men are, that they might have joy." (2 Nephi 2:25.) But our assigned work must come before almost everything, and how we do it contributes greatly to our mental, physical, financial, and moral health. Most of us would not stay healthy or happy for very many pay days if any or all of our business should stop.

## Sickness and Health

People's attitudes about health have undergone many changes over the course of history. Before science proved otherwise, illness was often thought of as the invasion of the body by evil demons. Recently there has grown up a great field of knowledge about our health called psychosomatic medicine, which says that many of the troubles that manifest themselves as physical symptoms have their origin in mental or emotional disturbances.

In one way or another, most people are sick. A person's physical health can be imperiled by certain emotions. If there is bickering and hatred among family members, we are socially sick. If our spiritual appetites degenerate, we become morally sick. If we are possessed by the evil forces of sloth and lethargy, then a whole crowd of troublesome complaints are turned loose upon us. Our emotions are tied up with our success in all areas of our endeavor; consequently, the primary concern of our business *is* our health.

Mental and nervous breakdowns are usually associated with emotional evils, and breakdowns attributed to overwork are usually caused by our attitude toward our work and our failure to achieve acceptable standards of excellence. When the evil spirits of frustration, hatred, weakness, and failure are eliminated from our work, then better health will result. Solomon said, "A merry heart doeth good like a medicine." (Proverbs 17:22.) A clear conscience and a sense of righteousness also doeth good like medicine.

## Some Origins of Disease

Dr. Karl Menninger of Topeka, Kansas, has said that more people in the United States are mentally ill than are hospitalized for all other diseases and illnesses combined. He says that it is not an overstatement to say that fully 50 percent of the problems of the acute stages of an illness and 75 percent of the difficulties of convalescence have their primary origin not in the body but in the mind of the patient. Work itself does not kill. Laborers do not usually die of heart attacks; it is more frequently the person who is laboring under some unnatural emotional stress where the frustrations and worries settle in his heart. Sickness can be the result of laziness, a guilty conscience, frustrations, and other factors that produce emotions beset with mental conflicts.

Most of these mental, and consequently physical, diseases begin with inertia, lack of planning, idleness, and the habit of running away from our problems. When we fail to study the great spiritual truths and when we fall down in our occupational responsibilities, then we are beset with a paralyzing ignorance, and a whole tribe of other evil spirits overwhelm us, including the demons of anxiety, fear, obsession, compulsion, delusions, hallucinations, illusions, and an array of physical complaints stemming from the mind. These are the counterparts of the well-known physical symptoms. When we form bad habits of work or develop unfavorable attitudes about our families, our religion, and our social responsibilities, over a few years time complexes, emotional deformities, and distortions of attitude result, all of which involve our relations with other people as well as our own feelings and personalities. If these weaknesses are allowed to go far enough, they can lead to mental, physical, and moral breakdowns.

Thus, when we say we're not in business for our health, we are just kidding ourselves. Everyone should be conscious of the fact that he is in business for his health, and he ought to work at it wholeheartedly.

## Run For Your Life

The story is told of an aviator in the Arctic Circle whose plane had crashed. He knew that there was help beyond the hills, but before he had gone very far, he felt a drowsy lethargy overpowering him and he felt that if he could lie down in the soft, warm snow and rest, everything would be all right. As he felt the comfort and peace of his snowy bed, it suddenly dawned on him that he was in the last stages of freezing to death. He jumped to his feet and began running for his life toward the hills, and it wasn't long before the warm blood was churning in his system. All of us are running for our lives, and if we keep our hearts pumping enough blood, we are safe, for while the heart continues to remain sound, all other sicknesses are superficial and temporary.

Our emotions might be compared to the engines of our automobiles. Usually we do not look under the hood until the car stops or begins to sputter, but at that late day, when we try to find and correct the problem, we frequently do not know what we are looking for. When the appendix becomes inflamed, we are warned of the fact by a lot of symptoms. We feel sick to the stomach, have no appetite, are constipated, and there is the pain in the abdomen. When we are working and living improperly, we also get some warning symptoms telling us that emotional trouble is imminent. Conflicts begin to arise. We have damaging feelings of guilt and inferiority. We start accusing others, and instead of meeting our problems squarely, we alibi, offer excuses, and think illogically. Then we begin falling down in our business and we may need psychiatric help.

### Hate and Anger Can Kill

When we are behind in our work, we always hate it. When we are ahead in our work, we always love it. If we abuse our work, we dislike it. If we abuse our families, we dislike them. If we cling to evil, we hate those things having to do with good.

Some time ago, a national magazine conducted a survey in which it was found that 75 percent of all people hate their jobs. If they just hated one job the solution would be simple, for they could quit that job and start one that they enjoyed. But, if we ourselves are sick, then we may not like the second job any better than the first, and the third may have just as many failings as the second.

When we get stomach ulcers from our family bickering, that part of our business is in serious trouble, and when we moan about how hard it is for us to live our religion, it is certain that we are not being very devoted to our Father's business. We should take steps to get a hold of all these problems before they get a stranglehold upon us. Any one of these serious emotions that develop because we are not doing our work well may invade the organs of our bodies and leave us with several kinds of sickness. Our hate and anger can kill us. Our sloth and lethargy and ignorance can ruin our lives. Our sins against our families can destroy our happiness. And the evil involved in our disobedience to God can destroy our souls.

How to Love Work

The mind and emotions are not immune to disorder, and we ought to learn to love our jobs. We learn to love our work by doing it well. Success is antiseptic — it kills all the germs of disease. Sigmund Freud spoke of creating an emotional cathartic, or a purgative medicine, to purify our systems by draining off our pent-up emotions from their unnatural incorporation in the organs of the body. This can best be done by genuine repentance, a turning away from evil, and then launching a vigorous quest for excellence and success in all aspects of our lives.

Disease is a fractional death, and the degree of our health determines the total effectiveness of our lives. The main thing for which we are in business is to have life and to have it more abundantly. So let's start this very day and be as businesslike as possible in developing a healthy mind, a healthy spirit, and a healthy personality, incorporated in a healthy body.

# Plans and Goals

# 16
# The Law of
# COMPENSATION

Everyone seeking success and happiness should maintain an intimate familiarity with the thrilling story of Ben Hur. Over 2000 years ago in the ancient city of Antioch, there was a young Jew by the name of Ben Hur who had been falsely accused of a crime and was sentenced to hard labor at the oars of a Roman galley. All day long he was chained to his bench. The galley oars were placed in his hands and a Roman whip was over his head. When his companions were rebellious or revengeful, they brought down upon themselves the lashes of their Roman masters. But Ben Hur was not rebellious, and he asked only that he be alternated from one side of the ship to the other so that his muscles might develop symmetrically.

### He Won Friendship and Self-Respect

Ben Hur did far more work than even his captors expected or asked, and every stroke helped to build a more perfect, a more beautiful, and a more powerful body. Not only did he grow physically strong, but his cheerful spirit and fine attitude also built up a winning personality. He won the admiration and friendship of his masters and his own self-respect.

## The Day of the Race

One day there was a devastating shipwreck and Ben Hur was able to save the life of the Roman tribune, and his heroism and excellence won for him his freedom.

Then came the day of the great chariot races. But, as the race was about to begin, it was discovered that one span of horses was without a driver. In desperation the aid of Ben Hur was sought, and the young ex-slave was begged to take the place of the missing driver. As he picked up the reins, a mighty cry went up from the onlookers, for never had they seen such mighty arms or such a powerful body. With great courage and confidence Ben Hur drove the charging horses to a notable victory and won great fame for himself.

There is an old axiom that points out that the Lord always fits the back to the burden. There seems to be a psychological mechanism in each of us that makes sure that every effort we make is compensated for; and frequently, when nature wants to make us great, she gives us some difficulty to strengthen our muscles or some deficiency to promote our resourcefulness.

## Rewards May Be Delayed

Many people would argue with this law, not believing its truth, because they have seen or experienced cases when compensation did not seem evident. Usually the only problem is that these people were not patient enough. How much compensation did Ben Hur receive prior to the shipwreck?

It seems as though all of our human talents are granted on a kind of lend-lease basis, and they grow best as they are used most and often the large and obvious rewards come on a delayed basis. However, when we fail to use our talents to their limit, we lose their growth correspondingly. Thus, to the exact extent that they are idle, life repossesses them.

A native manifestation of this law is encountered when one ties his arm up in a sling and sees his muscles disappear.

Nature's law of compensation does not merely work in multiplications and additions — it also involves some subtractions. Even Ben Hur had to pay a kind of muscle maintenance charge in order to keep possession.

## Rewards Are Sure

Ralph Waldo Emerson wrote a great many things about this interesting law of compensation. He pointed out that for every act there is an appropriate compensation. Just as no one can do any good thing without at some time, in some way, receiving a reward, so no one can do an evil thing without suffering a penalty. The cause and effect, the means and the end, the seed and the fruit cannot be separated. The effect already blooms in the cause, and the end always breeds in the means. The fruit is already hidden in the seed.

Emerson teaches the lesson of Ben Hur when he says that if we serve an ungrateful master, we should serve him the more. Build up our balances and put God in our debt, for it is the law that every stroke shall be repaid. The longer the payment is withheld, the better for us, for compound interest on compound interest is the rate of usage under this magnificently profitable law. We get paid back in kind multiplied. The negative portion of this law is just as certain: Curses always recoil upon the heads of those who imprecate them. The chickens come home to roost. One cannot do wrong without suffering wrong. And the thief always steals something from himself.

Every time we try to hoard an ability or withhold a service, something is taken from us. As we acquire new arts, we sometimes lose old virtues. As we have built up our means for effortless transportation, many people have lost the full use of their feet. When we support ourselves with various kinds of crutches, our muscles themselves lose their strength. A notebook may impair our memory. Labor-saving devices make us weak. Those entertainments outside ourselves leave us bored and eventually incapable of amusing ourselves. In many ways we become weaker by every recruit that we enlist under our banner.

## Can Life Cheat You?

Some men suffer all their lives from the foolish superstition that life is cheating them. However, it is impossible for a man to be cheated by anyone except himself. Some people try to do just as little work as possible and still get by, and that is about all they ever do get. Many people want to be paid before they give the service. They want to receive favors and render none. They want to get out of life all that the traffic will bear. These people are only cheating themselves.

Mr. Emerson says that we should "work every hour, paid or unpaid; see only that you work, and you cannot escape the reward." No matter how often we are defeated, we will succeed if we keep vigorously and enthusiastically trying.

## The Numbers Game

Anyone who wants to be successful should absorb the numbers game into his life. If you want to be a success, you must be willing to make the necessary investment.

The numbers principle applies, of course, in every aspect of life. Take book publishing, for instance. Erich Segal taught at Harvard for years, and prepared some scholarly research articles. In a sudden turnaround, he wrote a sentimental, romantic novel. He sent the book off to a publisher and awaited the reply. It must have been galling to receive a noncommital rejection notice from that first company.

There are undoubtedly thousands of authors, unacquainted with the numbers game, who pack their stories away forever after one rejection notice. Segal, however, sent his novel on the rounds of the publishing houses.

In all, that novel was turned down many times before Hollywood discovered it. The novel was made into a film entitled *Love Story* and was published in book form as well. The film was a box office sensation and made its delighted author a regular fixture on TV talk shows. Needless to say, *Love Story* made a lot of money for Erich Segal. He had been willing to make the numbers investment. He made not one try, but dozens, in order to increase his chance for success and the result — compensation.

Everyone was born to happiness and victory. No effort is ever wasted or lost. Even the galley slave can get satisfaction out of his work when he performs it on the highest activity level. Of course, we should not be impatient if the books are not balanced every Saturday night. To really understand and wholeheartedly believe in this great law of compensation is one of the best stimulants for forming a powerful, winning attitude and bringing about a productive satisfying success.

## The Second Mile

It will pay to be Ben Hur kinds of people. These types of individuals always try to do more than they get paid for, and then they get paid for more than they do. They try to put more back into life than they take out. These people always go the second mile. They never worry about the pay or who gets the credit. To them it is far more important to think of the good they may do and the service they may perform.

In your current job or in any activity in which you are engaged, do more than is necessary. If you are given an assignment or a project, complete it to the best of your ability and then go beyond the scope of the task and complete it before a deadline, or submit related material, opinions, suggestions, or analysis.

Tell clients or your superiors that you indeed have their interests at heart and that their concern is your concern. Then prove that to them by above average effort and excellent performance. The important thing to remember is that no effort is ever lost.

Those things you acheive and learn by doing that which is not required will not only be a source of satisfaction to you, but when the time comes for promotions and bonuses the rewards will be as great, if not greater, than the satisfaction.

There is an unerring law of attraction to the effect that,

like Ben Hur, each of us will automatically draw to himself the exact reward that he has earned. This was the philosophy of Emerson, and it is also an immutable law of success.

# Plans and Goals

# 17
# The Law of
# VISION

One of the most thrilling stories in the New Testament tells of a blind man named Bartimaeus who begged for his living by the roadside just outside the city of Jericho. When he heard that Jesus of Nazareth was about to pass by, he began calling to him. Jesus heard Bartimaeus and asked that he be brought. Then Jesus said to him, "What wilt thou that I should do unto thee?" The blind man had asked for many things from many people as they had come down this road from Jericho, probably none of which had any great value. But this time he didn't ask for some small thing. When Jesus said, "What wilt thou that I should do unto thee," Bartimaeus replied, "Lord, that I might receive my sight." (See Mark 10:46-52.)

That is the thing we need more than anything else in the world. We need vision; we need understanding; we need appreciation. We don't see far enough, clearly enough, or soon enough.

Vision, the ability to see, is usually thought of as being a physical quality, but eyes are merely the instruments of sight. Sight itself is in our judgment, our understanding, our imagination. There are many things in a mountain range, for example, that may be visible to a geologist but that would remain unseen to one whose mind lacks the necessary knowledge or vision. One of the most common of experiences is to meet those "who have eyes but see not."

## Look and Plan Ahead

Vision probably has its most important aspect when we think of it as a quality of personality. Few people can look objectively and clearly beyond the boundary of their present circumstances. If an automobile could shine its light only one foot ahead of the radiator cap, a crack-up might reasonably be expected on a dark road at night. Such shortness of vision in human beings gives the same promise of trouble ahead. One of the greatest elements of safety in human personality, therefore, is that ability to look and plan ahead, and the value of this quality is in proportion to the clearness of the visibility and the range of the vision.

Many people are severely handicapped by shortsightedness. This not only jeopardizes security but also impairs usefulness and limits success. Many otherwise capable people are unable to look ahead or to contemplate those future circumstances that come outside their own experiences or the circle of their present needs. When one has his eyes focused too much on the present, the future tends to be blotted out of the vision. The story is told of the man who sold his bed of straw in the morning and then came back in the evening tearfully pleading to get it back, not having foreseen that he would need it again.

## In The Image of His Maker

Vision causes some of the greatest differences between people. The person who has vision thinks about and prepares for the future, while the person who lacks vision lives each day as it comes. One of the differences between humans and animals is that animals live only in the present. They walk on all fours with their eyes usually directed to the ground. Their vision is confined to a horizon of a few paces. By contrast, a human being stands upright in the image of his Maker so that he might look up to God and righteousness and eternal life. Our vision may reach the stars and bring back to us all the beauty and harmony of the universe.

The old maxim still applies that "where there is no vision, the people perish." We should develop the ability to project our plans and hopes beyond the boundary of our present circumstances.

## Use Your Imagination

One of the functions of the imagination is to help us transport ourselves into the future so that we can prelive events before we actually experience them. We can anticipate marriage, business opportunities, family situations, an improved personality, death, and even eternal life. The imagination compounds and mixes our own experience with the experiences of others and adds reason, hope, and faith to give us a picture of our future. This combination of virtues adds up to give us vision.

By virtue of our knowledge and good judgment, we can develop faith in our imagination until we have the actual experience. Imagination is one of the main ingredients of vision. The greatest areas of pleasure and pain, hopes and fears, both present and future, come by reason of our ability to see ahead. The quality of our vision is enhanced by our taste, the things we hope for, the amount of our industry, and the kind of person that we desire to become.

We can't afford to wait until the event takes place to prepare for it. If one waits to make an investment until all the reports are in and he knows what the profit will be, it may then be too late. In trying to see into the future, we should remember that there is an optical illusion in everybody which makes things close by look large and important, whereas things at a distance look small and insignificant. We have learned to make allowance for this phenomenon so far as physical eyesight is concerned. We are not fooled by the fact that the telephone pole by which we are standing seems very large and the one on the distant horizon seems like a pinpoint by comparison. The imagination however, is capable of running ahead and focusing the spotlight on the future so that it stands out like a beacon to light our way. Vision means light. The more light we can get on the objective, the better.

## Now I See

In the list of personality qualities we need to develop, we ought to include vision. One of the greatest causes of distress in life is shortsightedness. We must learn to look ahead, to think in terms of the future, and to learn to compensate effectively for the illusion that makes distant objects look unimportant. Then when we finally reach the horizon and look back, we will understand that the future has now become the most important of all. Vision says, "I see it." Faith says, "I believe it." Industry says, "I will achieve it."

One of the greatest of all accomplishments is to be able to say, as did the blind man, "Whereas I was blind, now I see."

# Plans and Goals

# 18
# The Law of
# WORDS

The painter works with color, the sculptor with form, and the musician with tone. Color and form and tone are beautiful and significant by virtue of what they are able to express, but they all fade into insignificance when compared with the power of speech. This is especially true in occupations in which speech is the instrument by which people also make their living. Automobiles run, airplanes fly, but most men literally talk themselves forward. Words are our most important tools, and one of the most effective ways of achieving success is to learn the meaning and shading and use of words.

A mediocre idea well expressed is often more effective than a better idea poorly expressed. Sir Winston Churchill's great leadership was largely based on his power of speech. Few men have understood the delicacies and luxuries of language better than he did; people read his works not only for what he says but for the way he says it. He met one crisis after another by his ability to express an idea with vivid imagery and tremendous force. These he prepared in advance — some of his neatly turned phrases are too smooth and perfect to be extemporaneous. But why shouldn't he prepare in advance? Napoleon didn't wait until the battle began to mold his cannon balls.

While facts constitute the material out of which arguments are made, yet passions, prejudices, sentiments, and the emotions play a strong part in determining the actions of human beings, and these are addressed, stimulated, and set on fire by the proper combination, shading, and expression of words and meanings.

## The Power In A Word

An unfortunate woman tramped through the empty streets of Paris at dawn one gray autumn day, starvation and despair in her eyes, mechanically tapping her drum and chanting, "Bread, bread, bread." She started the French Revolution in 1789.

Mark Antony took the Roman Empire away from Brutus and his fellow conspirators by the power of the words he uttered at the funeral of Caesar. Lawyers win cases, ministers save souls, statesmen make history, and salesmen make sales by the effective use of words. The quality of the idea and the effectiveness of its expression determine what will happen in the minds of those who listen.

Persons who are engaged in such business as teaching, leading, selling, politics, and other forms of persuasion and motivation ought to read and study logic, debate, rhetoric, literature, drama, language, poetry, all of which have to do with the effective understanding and use of words. Socrates used words to throw his listeners into perfect ecstasies. One who reads poetry must respond to its mood and stretch his mind to its widest dimensions. Great poets have stood next to the prophets in their ability to influence our lives. They have been persons whose imaginations have dared to leave the ground and ascend high enough to enable them to take a broader view of things. By the witchery of its music and radiance of its imagery, poetry gives pleasure to a leisure moment as well as helps us to master the art of word combinations.

## The Word Is Mightier Than Weapons

The evocative power of words is the secret of the poet. It is the secret of sales motivation. It wins for the lawyer and the politician. It is especially potent when there is added to it the influence of the character of the one who is using the words. Even a nod from a person who is esteemed is of more force than a thousand agruments or studied sentences from others.

It was said that Demosthenes was the best orator of his time, but Phoecian was the most powerful speaker. Commenting on the effect of these two speakers, when one spoke the people said, "How well Cicero speaks," but when Demosthenes spoke, they said, "Let's take up arms against Caesar." Zeno said that a philosopher should never speak until his words have been steeped in meaning.

The force of words can do more than can ever be done by conquering swords. Pyrrhus used to say that Cineas had taken more towns with his words than he had with arms. It is easy to overcome the bodies of those whose spirits have already been defeated.

It was said of Pericles that he wielded a dreadful thunderbolt from his tongue, and thunder and lightning resulted when he harangued. Others have been said to have such powerful use of words that they cut or hiss or pierce or burn. Words may also be used to soothe and comfort and heal.

The chief business of speech is to address the affections, the passions, the prejudices, and the ideas and feelings of men. What great power there is in the tongue if it is properly trained, especially when it is backed up by the reputation of a life and character free from every kind of corruption and taint.

Prepare To Speak

One experienced sales manager of an earlier day, wrote to an agent as follows:

Dear Agent: John Barrymore is an actor of long experience and great ability. How long would his reputation continue if he spoke extemporaneously and at random instead of giving the same old Hamlet speech that never fails to get across its message? Jane Cowl is one of the best Juliets ever to play the part. She says the same words the thousandth night as she did the first night, and people gladly pay five dollars to hear her. No one has yet succeeded in improving the wording of the Sermon on the Mount or the Gettysburg speech. Robert Ingersoll's address at his brother's grave brings the same emotions today that it did when first spoken. Wellington's appeal to his soldiers before the battle of Waterloo — well, read it. I ask you with all the earnestness at my command to prepare or adopt an already prepared, standardized canvass, one for each type of prospect — say four canvasses in all. They will make you money just as they made money for Jane Cowl and Barrymore and Bryan.

Study the word combinations of men like Winston Churchill. During the Battle of Britain he said, "Let us . . . so bear ourselves that, if the British Empire and its Commonwealth last for a thousand years, men will still say, 'This was their finest hour.'"

**Read More**

Statesmen have achieved greatness by the power and effectiveness of their speech. They are able to dominate and lead the will of their followers by the power of language. To help us develop greater word power we need to read more. We need to read the words of great men. We need to re-think their great thoughts and make them our own. As we make their words and thoughts our own, we will begin to receive great power. Our words, powerfully spoken will begin to have great influence on others. People will listen and follow our directions.

You will find yourself climbing quickly up the ladder of success if you develop your ability to effectively use words to influence and motivate people.

The greatest weapons men have are the weapons of their speech. Someone has said, "The pen is mightier than the sword." We carry on the contest for success with the weapon with which we should excel, our speech. Words effectively used are the magic carpet on which we fly to success.

# Plans and Goals

# 19
# The Law of
# PERSPECTIVE

The law of perspective includes that condition which makes everything close by look large and important and everything distant look small and unimportant. For instance, when one looks down a long row of telephone poles, the pole by which he is standing seems very large and impressive and the one on the distant horizon is just a pinpoint and very insignificant and unimportant.

That seems to be true, your eyes tell you that it is true, and yet it isn't true for if you get into your automobile and drive to the horizon and look back, you discover that the one by which you are now standing, which you thought of no consequence, is the most important of them all.

This important law emphasized the fact that things are not always as they seem. There are many optical illusions in life which cannot be detected by the sight or understood by the reason. For example, if you were standing in the middle of the desert and someone asked you what the shape of the earth was, if you relied upon your sense of sight, you would have to answer that it was flat and that the sun revolved around it. That also appears to be so.

There are some things where not only our senses deceive

us but our reason is just as useless. For example, supposing you were born fully matured with your reason at its height, but lacking actual experience. Then supposing two cubes were set in front of you, one was glass; the other ice. At the distance of one foot you may not be able to tell the difference. There is no possible power of reason or eyesight to tell you that one of these is the result of heating sand and the other the product of freezing water.

**There are Many Ways of Seeing**

One of the important laws of success is to learn that certain impressions and evidences must be "weighed" and "shaded" in one way or another if the proper judgment is to be had. The law of perspective might be illustrated by the story of the six blind men from Hindustan who went to see the elephant. The one who took hold of the elephant's tail thought the elephant was like a rope, the one who felt the broad side of the elephant decided the elephant was like a wall; the one who stood by his leg thought the elephant was like a tree, and the one who took hold of his trunk thought the elephant was like a snake. Their point of view, or perspective, gave each an entirely different impression.

There is a story of a wise Indian chief who required that before one of his braves could qualify to sit in his judgment council he was required to walk for three days in the moccasins of the man on trial. How different our point of view becomes when we are in the other man's shoes.

We sometimes worry about problems which, because of our nearness to them, have an importance all out of proportion to fact, and we often give no importance at all to something if it lies a little bit in the distance, either in time or space. If you put a quarter close enough to your eye, it will blot out of your vision the largest star, and if you put a half dollar over your eye, it will completely obliterate the sun which has a diameter of 866,000 miles.

There is also a part of the law of perspective which sometimes makes a prospective college student say, "Don't tell me about what I'm going to get in twenty years from now. The only thing I'm interested in is what I get right now." When a discouraged medical student can't see down the road a few years, we say he is shortsighted. This deception in perspective is the thing that got a Bible character named Esau into trouble.

## The Future Will Come

Esau came home one night hungry and said to his brother Jacob, "If you will give me a mess of pottage right now, I will assign over to you my birthright."

To one who had just had a good dinner, that would not have been a very attractive offer, but Esau was hungry and I suppose that he thought, "What difference does it make what happens ten years from now, I am hungry right now." I don't even know what a mess of pottage is, it doesn't sound very appetizing to me, but Esau traded his entire birthright to get it. And this same problem of deception is still with us in many varied forms.

When we are at the beginning of any worthwhile project, the little problems that we run up against sometimes seem monumental in size; whereas the thought of ultimate success, of honorable prestige and great accomplishment seem so far away as to be of no relative significance. But when one stands on the horizon of life and looks back, he will then know that the telephone pole that he thought insignificant has now become by far the most important of them all, while the little problems and difficulties that he had in the beginning he cannot now even remember, except in amazement that he ever gave them a second thought.

This law of perspective is tremendous in its effect upon our attitude and the enjoyment and appreciation that we have in our work, and while we are holding on to the elephant's tail, we ought to develop the ability to see as clearly as possible that he also has a trunk.

## Magnifying Glasses Help

Anyone working for success would do well to remember that things are not always what they seem. The world is not flat as it appears; it is round. It is not standing still as it seems to us; it is hurtling through space at a tremendous rate. The telephone pole on the horizon is not really inconsequential as it seems; it is the biggest telephone pole in the entire system. The people about us are not small and inconsiderate while we are big and generous. The sun is not smaller than a half dollar, and the twentieth year of our medical practice is not insignificant as compared with the first year. Fortunate is the man who trains himself to see things in their proper form and size, even though they are on the horizon of time or space.

We must learn to make compensation for the law of perspective. We might try using magnifying glasses when we give consideration to things of great importance or things in the future. A magnifying glass does not make an object larger, but it does make it seem larger and gives it back the importance it deserves so we can see it plainly enough to deal with it effectively.

# Plans and Goals

# 20
# The Law of
# EXAGGERATION

In many ways the business of life is "funny business" filled with contrasts and various shades of challenge and meaning. Manufacturing can be done on formula; chemical reactions can be put down on paper; they never change. But to write the directions of human success or any kind of personal achievement is not quite so simple. Sometimes people succeed where we can't explain their success and others fail where the formula says they should have succeeded. The personality factors that determine our success are made up of many parts; each has been included by creation for a helpful purpose, though we may not recognize the functions served by a particular quality.

## Exaggeration Serves A Purpose

For example, we have often heard that the trait of exaggeration is undersirable. But a quality that is so prominent in human nature must have been put there for a good purpose. There are areas where the ability to exaggerate is very helpful if its constructive function is understood.

For example, the schoolteacher writes on the blackboard with enlarged letters so that those in the back of the room can see and understand. A scientist looks at bacteria through a powerful microscope that increases the size of the bacteria by a few million times in his eyes. The Microscope does not actually make the bacteria larger; it only makes them appear larger so the scientist can work with them more effectively. Astronomers look through telescopes that not only enlarge the planets studied, but obligingly bring them a few million miles closer as well. The planet does not actually come closer; it only seems closer. It is an optical illusion, but it is a very helpful one.

People have developed great convenience and efficiency for themselves by putting bifocal glasses on their eyes. When they look at something close they look through one part of the glass; when they want to see something in the distance they look through another part.

## A Natural Tendency

The natural inborn tendency in human beings to exagerate shows up early in life. If you want an indication of the tendency to exaggerate, put your tongue into the cavity of your tooth. The tongue improperly reports to the brain that the cavity is many times larger than it actually is. Children usually live in a beautiful imaginary world where things are enlarged or contracted by them to suit their convenience, and the parents and homes of the chilren are given an important magnificence that can lift them up to God. If we look at our own children and compare them with others, it is natural to see our own many times fairer than anyone else's.

Isn't it strange that everyone in the world is great and good and fair in the eyes of some people though they may be extremely small and undesirable in the eyes of others? Wouldn't it be a humdrum life if we saw our own children or our own goals through the same eyes with which we look at our neighbors' children or our neighbors' goals? Charles Dickens once said that everyone should think well of his own business and everyone should also think well of God and his family and himself. That usually involves some enlargements of the ordinary.

## Rose-colored Glasses

Because nature has provided us with the wonderful

ability to see things in different lights, according to our interests, the mind becomes all-powerful and, as John Milton observed, "can make a heaven of hell or a hell of heaven." The young wife filled with attitudes of love and ambition can see her struggling husband as Sir Galahad in glistening armor, and he may behold her through the dishwater as a fabled and sabled princess. To reverse this process can create a very hell on earth.

Just think of the thrill and excitement the ability to exaggerate can give to what otherwise might be an ordinary existence. You remember Alfred Lord Tennyson's story of the knight, Sir Launfal. He gave up wealth, comfort, friends, family, and position and spent his life in search of the Holy Grail. He often had nothing to eat and had to sleep on the ground, but always before his eyes was the shining vision of the enlarged object of his quest which led him on with joyous and happy heart, making his life a thrilling adventure with dreams to harmonize.

The quality of exaggeration with a vivid imagination helps us to paint pictures and dream dreams to correspond with our hopes. The importance of life is sometimes painted in drab colors and life's music is tuned down to seem ordinary and unexciting. We need the ability to look at the world through rose-colored glasses, and give life the importance that it will have when we see it in the light of eternity.

### Accentuate the Positive

Much of success consists in knowing which things to exaggerate and which to reduce in size. If we look at an object through one end of the telescope it looks very close and very large; if we look through the other end it looks very distant and very small. Our success depends largely on our skill in knowing which end of the telescope to use on any given occasion.

If one would like to be a happily married man, he should look at his wife's virtues through the end of the telescope that magnifies, but always look at her faults through the little end of the telescope. By this process virtues become mountains and faults become molehills.

The story is told of an Arabian sheik who looked at the figs he was having for dinner through a magnifying glass, and the figs seemed to be crawling with all kinds of horrible looking little bacteria. This spoiled his present and future dinners, because he had no way of knowing that these startling forms of bacteria were placed there in his interest. Many of the problems and disciplines of life are also given for our benefit; sometimes they are most productively utilized by looking at them through the little end of the telescope, and sometimes we need to tune out the vision altogether. On the other hand, we ought to amplify the vision of our faith so we can see across the boundaries of mortality to the future scenes as they will someday appear in reality.

### Few Would Trade

Our inspired imaginations give us a supermortal picturing power wherewith we can enlarge our objectives and make ambitions and pleasures more intense and meaningful. Many people in the most ordinary situtations live in the presence of angelic music and colorful visions. This quality enables the most humble person to see his own objectives as well as himself multiplied in importance and destiny and greatly increased in fascination. On the other hand, we see other people in an entirely ordinary light. Very few people have ever indicated a desire to trade circumstances with anybody else. No matter how bad off we may be, it is common for us to see our troubles less and our pleasure more than those of other people.

Some people may think that to deliberately change the size of things we present to our minds and emotions is a form of misrepresentation. Actually it is not, for as Paul says, "For now we see through a glass, darkly" (1 Corinthians 13:13), and exaggeration helps us to lighten things up and to see them as they will sometime actually be. The microscope of the doctor is a justifiable misrepresentation made for the benefit of everyone. So is the telescope of the astronomer.

### A Tool For Happiness

There is a means by which we may enlarge our personal

success and happiness. The family has been the basic unit of society and the starting point for most of our love, happiness, and education; and if our family success is increased, our happiness and personal welfare are greatly magnified. It is not necessary that the intensity of the love of a parent for his child should be shared by others. Therefore, even from an impartial point of view, the parent's feelings for the child are not a misrepresentation, and yet they contribute vastly to the happiness of those participating.

A good cook is one who makes ordinary things extraordinarily delightful. A great artist or sculptor or writer is one who makes ordinary things more beautiful. A musician can put the measured, metered, and rhymed words of a poet together with his musical ideas and create a song.

The effective, judicious use of the ability to enlarge upon our benefits and reduce our problems is probably the greatest single source of happiness. A little girl said that her grandfather always put on his red glasses when he ate cherries because it made the cherries seem so much bigger and redder than they actually were. If we owned a famous painting, we would certainly hang it where it would get the best possible light to add to its beauty and importance. To always put our best foot forward may also be a very worthwhile form of misrepresentation.

### Mountains and Molehills

Some unhappy people reverse this process, always with disastrous results. They fight their jobs; they look at their employers through the wrong end of the telescope; they tear down heroes; and when they say "Tell it as it is," they mean to magnify the worst instead of the best. They make molehills out of virtues and mountains out of faults. Some people even look at themselves through the belittling end of the telescope, which produces so much discouragement and despair that life itself seems not be be worthwhile, because virtues appear as molehills and faults become towering mountains.

The dictionary says that to exaggerate is to present

extravagantly, to increase immoderately, to heighten unduly, to magnify, to glorify, to increase the force, strength, or intensity of. What a constructive direction that is for making the best and the most of our own lives!

Enthusiasm, cheerfulness, and good attitudes grow out of our satisfactions, and because the tendency to exaggerate was put in our nature for our benefit, we ought to learn how to use it to the best advantage. How inspiring to see a doctor or a teacher or a salesman who has extraordinary love for what he is doing and those whom he serves and who exaggerates in his own mind the importance of his calling. A little of this kind of exaggeration in the right places makes everyone more enthusiastic, more devoted, more capable, more happy.

### Reduced Discouragement

On the other hand, what great benefits are born when one turns the little end of the telescope on the slights, bickerings and the unpleasant things that are best forgotten as quickly as possible. The man working for success should look at his troubles and obstacles through the little end of the telescope to reduce discouragement.

The freedom to exaggerate is one of the great freedoms, and to know when to reverse the telescope is like painting a great picture; it's a fine art. It is one of the greatest good fortunes of our lives that we may enlarge to our heart's content the importance of those things that are good for us and will bring us eternal life and eternal happiness, and blot out our attention to those things that otherwise would draw us down.

# Plans and Goals

# 21
# The Law of
# GROWTH

The law of growth is the law of struggle. It is the process of overcoming obstacles. If you want to develop a strong back, get a heavy load to carry. Life is made up of opposites, and our motivation is the way we overcome inertia.

## The Struggle Itself

It is said that to enable us to solve our problems, God always sends the remedy before the plague, and into human nature he has put the power to grow, which is the power to struggle. It is the struggle itself that pleases us far more than the victory. We love to see a prize fight. We do not enjoy seeing an infuriated victor oppress the vanquished, but when we see the victorious end, we are satiated.

Suppose that all your objectives in life could be immediately realized. Suppose that you could meet the foe, fight the battle, and overcome once and for all in a single encounter. Suppose that all of the races could be won and all of the blue ribbons hung on the wall and all the progress could be completely effected and recorded at this very instant. There would be great joy and happiness now, but the future would probably be filled with boredom and discontent. Happiness comes while we are in pursuit of an important objective. If the means has ceased to charm, then how could there ever again be any interest in the end? Strife is necessary to victory. We often do not seek things for themselves alone, but for the joy we have in the search.

In a play, scenes that do not arouse the emotions of challenge and accomplishment lose much of their possible joy. People do not gamble for money; they gamble for the thrill of winning. Pursuit is better than possession. Men do not chase a rabbit for the food. In fact, the hungry person would be insulted if you were to offer him a dead rabbit as a gift. It is the pursuit, the chase, the hunt, the conquest that pleases. That is one of the reasons why imprisonment is such a horrible punishment. A prisoner is not going any place. People seek satisfaction in struggle against difficulty, and when they have conquered, rest becomes insufferable. Nothing makes governments or individuals so careless as the knowledge that there will be no opposition to their acts. Both teachers and learners go to sleep at their post as soon as there is no enemy in the field. Only the conquest pleases. The pleasure of bragging tomorrow among one's friends that one has played better than another is motive enough.

Those who do not persist in struggle do not grow and are marked for early elimination. The weak and the strong, the rich and the poor, the ignorant and the well-informed are continually changing places. Someone has said that we should always be kind to those whom we pass up on the way to success, because we may pass them again on our way down. The only way that anyone has ever been known to coast is downhill. The grass looks greener on the other side of the fence because nature is trying to entice us forward. She is trying to stimulate our appetite for the chase. She is trying to intrigue us not to give up the fight.

To overcome the power of inertia, we have been given a restlessness in our natures. We want to get something a little better. We drop one thing as soon as it has been attained and start something else. We have been given an upward reach; this ability to grow constitutes the godlike instinct that creation has placed within us.

## The First Ascent

Life is like the climb up the mountainside. We start at the bottom and what then appears to us to be the top of the mountain is only the top of the first ascent, for when we reach the top of this level, we see another length of mountain reaching out and beyond it. Even so, when we accomplish any one thing, we always see a new objective spreading ahead of us. It is our nature never to be fully satisfied.

As long as we can keep this climbing characteristic within us active, we are safe. We should find some effective way to help nature by constantly stimulating ourselves. There may be a question in our minds about using some physical stimulants, but mental and spiritual stimulants are necessary to growth, and the more habit-forming they are, the better. It's a part of the principle that if we are not going forward, we will slip backward. When we stop being better, we stop being good. When one avoids struggle, he soon finds that he has changed places with someone who used to play on the second team but who has a stronger struggle urge within him.

## Keep On Your Feet

It has been said that necessity is the mother of invention. Necessity stimulates our stuggle, and one who relaxes in the struggle is soon eliminated. There is great wisdom in the fact that man is born to struggle. Like the man freezing in the snow, we should keep going. To stop and lie down in a blizzard or in life is the worst thing one can do. No matter what other shortcoming one may have, if he'll just keep on his feet and keep moving in the right direction, he may hope to someday arrive at his destination, and everything will turn out all right.

# Plans and Goals

# 22
# The Law of
# DESIRE

Suppose that you were going to try to build a successful football team. Can you think of any one quality that you would rather have in those who were going to be your players than an intense desire to win? Here's a man whose whole heart is in his job of carrying the ball. He is so determined to succeed that if you cut his head off, he might still keep on going. His desire is not only in his brain; it is also in his tissues, his muscles, and his nervous system. If he has a fighting heart and a passion to win, his success is half won.

## Get Hot

Desire is said to be like the heating process that takes place inside the hard shell of a black walnut. When the life inside the black walnut starts to heat, no power can hold it. It breaks open the stone-like shell as if it were paper. It sends up a shoot through the black earth toward the sun to eventually become a great walnut tree. When we get hot inside something is bound to happen.

Everything else is secondary to a will to win. Senator Reed Smoot once said that an ambition to excel is indispensable to success. To excel one must have will — plus. Mostly will is desire, but desire is also a great many other things.

I once had the presiding officer of a group of missionaries say that when he had someone under his direction who was over forty years of age, he was never required to memorize. And yet there are people in their sixties, seventies, and eighties who can memorize faster than when they were in their twenties.

It may not be that the brain itself is more retentive, but the older person's interest and desire may be greater. That is, if you have an inch of brain and a foot of interest, you will do much better than if you have a foot of brain and an inch of interest. There are few things more difficult than for even the most intellectual man to memorize something that he doesn't want to know. It is an interesting fact that creditors have a much better memory than debtors.

### The Freedom to Want

When we desire anything strongly enough, we are usually able to develop the will to secure it. When one really desires to be successful, he is not far from actually being so. Strong impulses create a mysterious kind of energy. If you can find a man with strong impulses, under the government of a strong will, he automatically has an energetic character and his success is assured. It has been said that freedom from want is one of the great freedoms; and yet more important is the freedom to want.

The football player who wants to win never notices the bumps, the bruises, the mud, or the obstacles. He has developed a philosophy of victory, a sort of mental auto-intoxication.

This is a productive kind of self-hypnotism, which transforms the fatigue and the cold and the bruises and the obstacles into a facinating, exhilarating series of thrills and satisfactions. These are facts well known to everyone, but only a few try to apply this powerful principle to their own lives. Yet we rarely succeed without it. We go through life an onlooker to success, rather than a participant.

The power of momentum which we create by a hot desire for success is one of the greatest forces in the world, greater than gravity, greater than dynamite. It has been said that geniuses tell in capital letters the same story that common folk tell in ordinary type. A midget desire even with a giant intellect usually spells failure.

### Hunger to Succeed

We should be careful about satisfying too thoroughly our hunger to succeed because then it may die. It is sometimes true that when some young men arrive too early at fame and repute, the early attainment is apt to extinguish their thirst (unless they continue to set higher goals!) and satiate their appetite; whereas the first success of more hungry characters stimulates and quickens them and takes them in still hotter pursuit of their contemplated success. They look upon these proofs of their abilities, not as recompense for what they have already done, but as a pledge given to themselves of what they will perform hereafter. It is like a tiger who gets a little blood on his nose — it inflames his appetite.

We must learn how to increase and intensify this desire and fan it into a passion. We should cultivate and aggravate and magnify our desires so that they assume an importance in our mind where we are willing to go after our objective with all our heart.

### Fan the Flame

There was an ancient tradition that Antony, the successor to Julius Caesar, was a descendant of Hercules. He was proud of his divine ancestor — the god Hercules, and wanted to be worthy of him. This gave him a motive. The motive that led Antony was the same that formerly led Alexander or Cyrus against all mankind. The unquenchable thirst of empire and the burning ambition of being the greatest man in the world can bring into play undreamed of resources, energy, and power!

These may be faulty motives, but whatever your objective in life is, learn to cultivate the *desire, dwell on its importance, magnify it in your own eyes, fan the flame until it becomes a forest fire. It is a natural law that whatever you desire intensely enough, life will wrap up and hand to you free of charge.*

## THE CHAMPION

The average runner sprints
Until the breath in him is gone,
But the champion has the iron will
That makes him carry on.
For rest the average runner begs
When limp his muscles grow,
But the champion runs on leaden legs,
His spirit makes them go.

The average man's complacent
When he has done his best to score;
But the champion does his best,
And then he does a little more.

# Plans and Goals

# 23
# The Law of
# MOTIVATION

The first step in any undertaking is to discover the problem. The biggest problem of everyone is the natural tendency toward a kind of human inertia. Inertia is the strongest power either in nature or in human beings. Everything falls downward out of its appetite for rest. Everything, including human beings, tends to stay put or if once set in motion, it quickly tends to come to a standstill. We know of no perpetual motion. And to be "inert" is to lack the inherent power to move overcoming inertia.

Motivation is that force which fights against and tends to overcome inertia. It is the power which gets us into motion. Human beings, like everything else, must be wound up occasionally.

Somebody indicated this weakness in our lives when he said:

> I wish I was a little rock
> A sittin' on the hill
> A doin' nothin' all day long
> 'Cept just a sittin' still
> I wouldn't eat, I wouldn't sleep
> I wouldn't even wash
> I'd sit and sit a thousand years
> And rest myself, by gosh!

And this appetite to be inert is one of the serious problems of our human world.

The great science of crime detection has been built around the law of motive. This law is to the effect that behind every act there is a motive. If the motive is known or can be discovered, the criminal can usually be identified. The successful detective always looks for motive. The science of crime detection is the science of motivation in reverse. The detective is supplied with the result and works backward to find the motive. The leader starts with a motive and works forward to the result.

If you want one word to express success in any undertaking, the word is *motivation*. We need to be able to stir ourselves up, to get ourselves going, to be able to give ourselves some good continuous booster shots, or as we sometimes call it, we need an occasional shot in the arm. Everyone knows enough to be a great success, but success is not knowledge; nothing is more common than unsuccessful men with knowledge.

## What Success Is Not

Success is not heredity; there are too many Abraham Lincolns. It is not environment; there are too many Booker T. Washingtons. It is not even aptitude; there are too many Demosthenes. Success is largely motivation.

Socrates said, "He who would move the world must first move himself." Solomon said, "With all thy getting, get understanding," and someone else who must have been even wiser than Solomon said, "With all thy getting, get going." This kind of action requires the ability to give ourselves a good kick from behind to get ourselves in motion. We know in detail every single thing we do to get ourselves where we want to go. (If you don't know specifically what you need to do by now, then start you own research and study program or subscribe to The International Journal of Success. See page 23.) We could all pass a high aptitude test in some particular thing. There is usually nothing the matter with the I.Q. of failures. The trouble with most of us is that we have just gone to sleep. We may have a high I.Q., or intelligence quotient, but a low M.Q., or motive quotient.

Our greatest fears should not be that life will someday come to an end, but rather that it will never really have a beginning. The ability to breathe the breath of life into our own machinery is one of the greatest abilities in the world.

## Success Must Have a Motive

Motivation first instructs and then animates. Mostly our greatest need is that the fires in our souls need rekindling. Fire will not burn without oxygen and success cannot exist in the absence of strong motive power. Without motivation, ambition is a weakling and imagination is rendered wingless. Every success must have a motive. Just as a watch must be wound up before it will run, so we need a technique keep our own mainspring tight and to keep our batteries charged. (At the expense of sounding over-confident, I'm quite certain that The International Journal of Success, referred to above will not only give you the very specific information you need in your quest for success, but more importantly, it will provide, on a regular basis, the necessary motivating power to insure that you keep on track until your goals are realized.)

There are two sections of this law of motivation. One has to do with motivating other people, but the most important part, certainly for us and the part with which this statement is concerned, is that part which has to do with motivating ourselves. The greatest sin against success is not in doing wrong; it is in doing nothing. We have a powerful tendency to procrastinate, to forget, to lose interest, to get lazy, to get discouraged, to get rusty. We have too many side interests which slow us down or get us off the track. With inactivity we soon lose confidence in our ability. We either lie down or sit down or fall down on the job.

A strong motivation is the power to break this deadly inertia. Thomas Huxley said the great end of life is not knowledge but action. So in planning our own success, we should test and strengthen our ability to motivate ourselves.

### The Causes of Failure Are One

Recently a survey was taken among the salesmen of a great company which indicated that out of one hundred failures,

37 failed because of discouragement
37 more failed because of lack of industry
12 failed because they did not follow instruction
8 failed because of lack of knowledge.

Discouragement is an attitude growing out of inertia. Lack of industry is inertia. The failure to follow instruction is an attitude, an offspring of inertia. Lack of knowledge is caused by inertia. All failed because they lacked sufficient motivation to overcome inertia.

### How Can We Overcome Inertia?

Dr. Henry C. Link says that "We should get physically active. We generate fears while we sit; we overcome them by action." Proper motivation corrects most of our problems. The great English Prime Minister Disraeli said, "The secret of success is constancy of purpose." And Elbert Hubbard said that "Genius is the power to make continuous effort." This is the ability to keep going in the right direction, which is the exact opposite of inertia.

Of course, the problem is, how can we overcome inertia? The answer may not be the same with any two individuals. One person responds to an entirely different stimulus than does another, but each must find ways to stimulate himself, and he should write out the factors by which he is effectively motivated. However, here are some good suggestions:

1. *Good Work* — It is a psychological law that we want to repeat those experiences which give us pleasure. There is no satisfaction that ever comes to a human being comparable to that which comes as a reward of accomplishment. When we

learn to do our job well we love it. When we do it poorly we hate it. Robert Louis Stevenson said, "I know what pleasure is for I have done good work." It follows naturally, therefore, that good performance is one of the strongest of motivators; therefore, always do good work.

2. *A Goal* — Most people never accomplish very much until they get in their mind a definite visual or written objective, the attainment of which is to them extremely important. Success is made up in part of the power to visualize the object. We must have a definite program on which we can compare our daily, weekly, monthly and yearly accomplishment.

3. *Records* — An effective goal is hardly possible without records to check up on ourselves. It is like driving in a race without a speedometer, or working to become a millionaire without the bank book. Without a record there is no way to know when we are on schedule. It is the score that makes the game. No athletic contest would be very interesting without a scorekeeper. This check-up also applies in everything else. Don't ever give your son an assignment without checking up on him, and it is even more important to check up on yourself. Set an objective, then have a definite system of record keeping and check-up from which you can determine progress. Live with the figures, think about them, let them agitate you.

4. *An Ambition to Excel* — We must WANT to succeed in capital letters. We are so constituted that we are greatly stimulated by the approval of others. We also like to think well of ourselves.

Vince Lombardi the famous football coach said that winning is not just the most important thing in athletics, it is everything in athletics; and it is also very important in life. The satisfaction of winning furnishes us with great motive power. What could be a stronger stimulant than to feel within ourselves that we are doing a good job.

5. *Reason* — Just think of the reasonableness of success. Think how many things depend upon your success, not only

your daily bread, but the welfare of your children, the kind of house you live in, the kind of car you drive, what happens in old age, what happens to your family at your death, your own security — almost everything you have and almost everything you are depends upon your success in your business. To fail just doesn't make sense or cents. It's unreasonable and it's stupid.

6. *Emotion* — The word emotion is very closely related to motivation. Mostly we act according to how we feel. We should train our feelings as well as our thoughts. Enthusiasm can be acquired. During the bitter days of the Civil War, Julia Ward Howe wrote those stirring words to the Battle Hymn of the Republic. One verse says:

> In the beauty of the lily
> Christ was born across the sea
> With a glory in His bosom
> That transfigures you and me.
> As He died to make men holy,
> Let us die to make them free
> For God is marching on.

It is said that the effect produced by this battle song upon the weary northern soldiers as they marched to war was the equivalent to a reinforcement of a hundred thousand additional troops.

### Gather Great Ideas

A little emotion injected into the heart and mind of man is a great motivator. A soldier might prepare himself for battle by reading war stories and thinking thoughts of heriosm and courage and patriotism. Ideas carry moods. We can change our mood by changing our ideas and imagination. Some men have scrapbooks of ideas, poems, or philosophies that stimulate and stir their imagination. We ought to read great poems and stories that inspire enthusiasm, impel determination and motivate accomplishment. We ought to gather and keep around us the material that gives us great thoughts and ideas and that will motivate and teach us how to motivate ourselves.

In 1923, Adolph Hitler sat in a prison cell in Germany. He was without money, without influence, without education, without friends. But he was writing in his book "Mein Kampf" his plan to make Germany the greatest nation in the world. The fact that starting out single handed, he almost upset the world indicated that he had something. We might ask ourselves, How did he do it? The answer is in his book. He said, "The question of Germany regaining her power is not how to manufacture or distribute arms, but how to produce in people that will to win, that spirit of determination, which produces a thousand different methods, each of which ends with arms."

### Direction Is Important

Hitler fought in a bad cause, but he understood and used the Law of Motivation. He knew that power is not in armaments, but in a highly motivated intelligent human personality, and he was able to work his own enthusiasm up to a white-hot pitch. We can do the same, but in addition we can keep our motivation directed toward worthwhile and worthy causes.

You see, anyone can use the immutable laws in this book, although it is quite unfortunate that many times these laws are used by unscrupulous people for destructive purposes. To counteract this, we must consistently and successfully apply these truths to help build rather than to destroy the world.

Our problems are like the problem of the three medical students who were trying to make a cadaver which they were studying stand up on its own feet against the wall. But each time, just as they seemed to have him balanced, he would slump down on the floor in a heap. One of the students observed, "I know what is the matter with this dummy, he hasn't any spirit in him." That is often the trouble of one who fails. He lacks spirit. He lacks enthusiasm. He lacks motive.

Motivation is an inside job. We should choose carefully our motives and then cultivate and agitate them while they drive us on to our projected success.

# Plans and Goals

# 24
# The Law of
# INNER RESOURCES

The greatest area for exploration, discovery, and development is not in the diamond mines or oil fields; nor is it the miracle of the machine or the splitting of the atom. It is rather something that is buried very deep in the human personality. *A human personality is the thing that gives value and significance to every other known resource.* None of the discoveries of science, or the inventions of the ages compare in significance with the essence that we call a human character and personality. Yet human personality is the thing we know the least about of anything in the world.

You can ask a man a great many questions about science, invention, history, or politics and he will answer you. But if you ask him to write out an analysis of himself, to tell you about his mind and soul qualities; if you ask him to describe the qualities of his personality or the power of his will, you may not get a very good answer. Men have learned to know the stars; we have learned to use the microscope and the telescope which has opened up vast new worlds of infinite importance. But man remains largely a mystery to himself. The undiscovered continent lies under the hat and within the soul of the average human being.

## Unexplored Territory

The whole field of intuition, instinct, revelation or inspiration is relatively unexplored and still lies mostly beyond the furthermost limits of the imagination. No man knows his total capacity for initiative or accomplishment. Genius is commonly developed in men by some deficiency that stabs them wide awake and becomes a major incentive. We only need to be sufficiently aroused.

Emerson believed that man becomes weak to the extent that he looks outside himself for help. When men developed watches, they largely lost the power to tell time by the sun. When the mole stopped using his eyes, nature took away his eyesight; and when we start depending on outside supports, our own power is diminished.

It is only as man throws himself unhesitatingly upon the powers within himself that he learns his own strength and is thereby able to work miracles of accomplishment. It is only when one throws overboard all other props and leans substantially upon the magic that our Creator has placed within each of us that he uncovers his real powers and abilities.

## A Kinship With God

Our instincts and emotions do not have to be taught, they are implanted before birth. They spring out of nature when the time is right. Then we feel and know. There seems to be a sense of divinity that is a part of every man. Great men especially often feel they have a kinship with God. A "universal life" seems to flow through them and they feel they are instruments of Deity.

The Hindus explain this marvelous piece of equipment called a human life with all its wonderful abilities by their belief in reincarnation. They believe that most of the things that men do and know are a result of knowledge acquired in a previous incarnation. It is certainly a fact that there are a great many things that we do not understand about ourselves. Men have tried to explain this in different ways. The poet, Wordsworth says:

> Our birth is but a sleep and a forgetting:
> The soul that rises with us, our life's star
> Hath had elsewhere its setting
> And cometh from afar:
> Not in entire forgetfulness,
> And not in utter nakedness,
> But trailing clouds of glory do we come
> From God, who is our home.

It is thought by some that at the time you were born you possessed more knowledge than is found in all the books in all the colleges and libraries of the world. Certainly it is true that we should not let any lack of academic training or formal education hold us back. It seems that man did pretty well before he had all the present-day educational opportunities. We should learn to rely more upon ourselves. Our minds seem to be equipped to meet every need.

### A Great Inner Reservoir

Many of the greatest men in the world were poor, uneducated men, with just the ordinary opportunities. Joan of Arc was a peasant girl, unable to read or write, yet she saved France. How did Beethoven become a great composer by age thirteen? Jesus was teaching wise men at age twelve. Who taught Edison or Shakespeare? Many great men have "discovered" truth which never before had been available in the world. It has been said that Lincoln was a child of nature, so close to the source of wisdom that he did not need to depend upon books or educators, or schools; for his brain and heart had access to the wisdom of the ages.

What you believe about how we got this way is relatively unimportant. The important thing is that we understand that every human being has a great inner reservoir of unseen ability which we may call forth to give us great power. We certainly should use this marvelous equipment of ours more. Homer said, "I consulted with my own great soul." That is what more of us should do more often.

The poet said:

Trust in thine own untried capacity
As thou wouldst trust in God himself;
Thy soul is but an emanation from the whole,
Thou dost not dream what forces lie in thee
Vast and unfathomed as the grandest sea.

No man can place a limit in thy strength;
Such triumphs as no mortal ever dreamed may yet be
     thine
If thou willst but believe in thy Creator and thyself.
At length some feet shall stand on heights now un-
     attained;
Why not thine own? Press on, Achieve, Achieve!!

It is often true that when a man is given every advantage he depends too much upon things outside himself and
does not rise to his possible expected height; whereas it is
sometimes true that the more circumstances conspire to
depress, the stronger becomes the urge of the life within you
for expression. It is the old case of the river that is dammed
generating more and more power as its accumulating force
builds up behind the dam. It is the irresistible head of steam
which makes success. That is why the blow which knocks all
the props from under us is often the turning point in our
whole career. We are then forced to develop our inner resources which, like an unused arm, we may have kept tied up
in a sling.

Suppose we believe that inherent in every man there is
a sense of divinity. Each has a kinship with God. The universal light flows through men and makes them instruments of Deity. Think what great power comes to us as
a consequence. Certainly it is true that a human being has a
greater dignity than he himself suspects.

It is certainly true that we know very little about ourselves. We discovered the orbits of the planets long before we
discovered the circulation of our own blood, and no one yet

knows much about the real elements of human personality. The greatest and most frequent mistake that is ever made by human beings is to under appraise the genius, the intelligence, and the tremendous possibility of ourselves.

# Plans and Goals

# 25
# The Law of
# INCREASING RETURNS

One of the most important discoveries of our world is made when we find out that we live in a world governed by laws. And we may make ourselves the beneficiaries of every one of the laws. One of the greatest of all success laws and one that we frequently overlook is the law of increasing returns.

In dictionary language, we might define this law by saying that an increase of labor or capital applied beyond a certain point causes a greater than proportionate increase in the production from the unit to which the additional labor or capital is applied. Or in simple terms, the person that works 10 percent harder (in the right way) should earn not 10 percent more but 20, 30, 50, or even 100 percent more.

Suppose that there were six elements determining your success. Suppose that you rated three on each of these success factors. Then suppose that by improvement you could increase your rating to four. Look what happens to the total:

$$3 \times 3 \times 3 \times 3 \times 3 \times 3 = 729$$
$$\text{but } 4 \times 4 \times 4 \times 4 \times 4 \times 4 = 4096$$

You increase each success factor only 33 1/3 percent and yet the total result is increased over five times.

That is, you don't need to be twice as good to double your score. If you are a third better, your score may be five times as great.

Douglas Malloch put this law of excellence into verse when he said:

> If you can't be a pine on the top of the hill
>     Be a scrub in the valley — but be
> The best little scrub by the side of the hill;
>     Be a bush if you can't be a tree.
>
> If you can't be a bush be a bit of the grass,
>     And some highway happier make;
> If you can't be a muskie then just be a bass —
>     But the liveliest bass in the lake!
>
> We can't all be captains, some have to be crew,
>     There's something for all of us here,
> There's big work to do and there's lesser to do,
>     And the task you must do is the near.
>
> If you can't be a highway then just be a trail,
>     If you can't be the sun be a star;
> It isn't by size that you win or you fail —
>     Be the best of whatever you are.

## Greatly Increased Rewards

Success has been compared to making a run in baseball. If you hit a three-bagger but die on third base, they don't count any part of it. But if you hit the ball a little harder and make a home run, you only did a little more work, but the reward is greatly increased. (And incidentally, the pay is much greater — in professional sports the stars and superstars are paid not 10 percent more but two, three, and five times more than the other guys that do *almost* as good a job.)

This law which says that the returns increase much faster than the amount of labor applied is in evidence all around us. For example, Armed was the race horse of the year in 1947. His earnings through 1947 were $761,500 and he later became the first thoroughbred in the history of United States racing to win a million dollars in prizes. The horse that finished close behind him time after time and sometimes only by a length or a nose in a mile, had earnings of approximately $75,000 dollars, and very few people ever heard his name. Do you think Armed was thirteen times as good or even twice as good? Actually, he wasn't even four percent better, and yet he earned thirteen times as much money.

The advantages of this important law of increasing returns might be further illustrated if we imagined ourselves as the Government and we were collecting income taxes. Out of the first thousand dollars we get $145. Out of the fifth one thousand dollars we would get $210. Out of the thirteenth one thousand dollars we would get $690, and out of the one hundredth seventieth thousand dollars, we would get $700. And that is the way it is in life. We usually do more work than we are paid for at the bottom of our condition, and we get more pay than we deserve when we put ourselves up at the top. If we never do more than we get paid for, we will likely never get paid for more than we do. Some people do as little as they possibly can to get by and that is about all that they ever do get.

The Parable of the Talents

Jesus is one of the chief proponents of this law of increasing returns. He told of a householder going into a far country and to one of his servants he gave one talent, to another five, and to another ten. When he returned, two of his servants had doubled his money, but the one to whom he gave one talent said, "I was afraid so I hid the talent in the ground and have earned nothing." Then Jesus said to the one who had been unprofitable, "Thou wicked and slothful servant." Then he said to those that were with him, "Take the talent from him and give it to him who hath ten talents and cast the unprofitable servant into outer darkness and there shall be weeping and gnashing of teeth." (Matt. 24:14-30.) Then Jesus said: "To him that hath shall be given, but from him that hath not shall be taken away even that which he hath." That is the law of increasing returns.

You remember in school that a seventy percent grade was passing. If you worked hard enough to get sixty-nine percent, you failed; but if you studied enough harder to get seventy-one percent, you passed. What a tremendous difference was made by that small extra effort. However, if you worked a little more effectively still, you may get close to one hundred percent. This small additional effort at the top of the scale can make you a real champion. And what great pleasure it is to be habitually and comfortably entitled to this permanent rank of superiority.

### The Razor's Edge

This magic law of increasing returns says that our income and our virtue and our happiness increase as we ascend the scale in excess of and out of proportion to the extra effort put forth to produce it. One person is just a little more thoughtful, plans a little better, works a little harder, stays at it a little longer, looks a little better, studies a little more, and he gets several times more credit, money, or world acclaim and fame.

Our business is the easiest and we have a lot more fun when we work the hardest. It is the hardest and we have a lot more headaches when we work the easiest.

A number of years ago, Daryl F. Zanuck made a four million dollar movie out of W. Somerset Maugham's book, *The Razor's Edge*. The point of the book has to do with the idea that the line that separates failure from success is as fine as a razor's edge.

One of the best illustrations of this truth was demonstrated in the filming of the picture itself. There were eight principal actors and eight stand-ins. That is, each principal had a substitute to do the hard, grueling, tiresome work. After the film was finished, *Life Magazine* published the pictures of the eight principals on one page and the eight stand-ins on the opposite page. The stand-in for Tyrone Power, for example, was Thomas Noonan, a close associate. They had gone through high school together. They were about the same size, equally intelligent, they were dressed about the same, and were very similar in appearance. As close a similarity as possible existed between each principal and his stand-in. But in one way, they were not similar. The combined salaries received by the eight principals for filming this picture amounted to $489,000 dollars. The combined salaries for the eight stand-ins amounted to $6,534 dollars. The principals were just a little bit better, but they received seventy-five times as much compensation.

Today, Marlon Brando is being paid over two million dollars for twelve days of play acting and I'm certain his stand-in won't make a fraction of that.

## Just a Ten Percent Difference

Just think of the magic that can be found in a mere ten percent. An ordinary man may stand seventy-two inches from the ground to the top of his head. Subtract ten percent and you have a runt. But if you add ten percent, you have a giant. Comparable changes take place when you subtract or add ten percent to your diligence or your perseverance or your enthusiasm or your faith. It makes a difference between a peewee and a giant.

As a result of this principle, we discover one of the secrets of leadership success. The outstanding leader is the one who does his best and then adds ten percent. He is the one who aims ten percent higher and works ten percent harder and stays on the job ten percent longer.

Some years back, a United Air Lines plane crashed into the top of Medicine Bow Mountain in Wyoming and sixty-five people lost their lives. The pilot was flying at 12,000 feet. If he had been flying at 12,055 feet, the lives of sixty-five people would have been saved. What a difference a few more feet in altitude would have made to those people and their families.

It is the same with our success. Often we fly just high enough to miss the tree tops. Whereas just a little more effort, a little more determination would put us in the big leagues of success in our business and our lives.

One of the greatest lessons of success is to go the extra mile. Do a little more and do with a little more faith, a little more energy, a little more go-at-it-iveness, and a little more stick-to-it-iveness, a little more devotion, a little more determination. And behold, you will have changed yourself from a stand-in to a star. The difference is just a little change in attitude and a little more effort in the right direction. The results are tremendous though the difference may be as fine as a razor's edge.

## Plans and Goals

# 26
# The Law of
# ATTRACTION

In China there are many unusual customs. If you visit in a Chinese home and let it be known that you greatly admire some particular article you see, the Chinese may wrap up that item and send it to you as a present. We would think this custom to be rather unusual, but isn't that exactly what life also does to us? There is a fundamental law of attraction that says, "That which we love and admire and desire we get." That is the way we get friends, character, and personality qualities as well as our material possessions. If we love honesty, we get honesty; if we love crime, we become criminals.

This is one of the most powerful of all laws governing the development of our characters and personality. If properly understood and developed, it has a tremendous cash value. The following is one application of this great idea.

## A Quest For Understanding

Elbert Hubbard wanted to make his own life as successful as possible. He read that Socrates had said, "Know thyself." He thought that the best way to learn about himself would be to study "human nature" as it manifested itself in other people. The study of human nature is the most fascinating of all knowledge. It gives us power, not only with others but it automatically helps us. Mr. Hubbard picked out 140 of what he considered the world's greatest men and then one at a time, over a period of fourteen years, he studied them carefully. He tried to discover what made them good or bad, successful or unsuccessful, loved or hated.

To make these impressions more definite, he wrote down his ideas in fourteen large volumes called, "Little Journeys Into the Lives of Great Men." We deepen our impressions and clarify our ideas by recounting them. He prepared these miniature biographies for his own personal benefit. For naturally, as he studied he would be attracted by certain qualities and would desire to have them for himself. And this law of attraction never fails. Those qualities that we love and desire and work for, life wraps up and sends to us as presents.

### The Story of Horatio Nelson

Inasmuch as this is the law, you might ask yourself what you would like. You may have your choice. Two of the cornerstones of success in our business, or in life, are *courage* and *industry*. Supposing you would like to strengthen these in yourself. Then read and think about them, fall in love with them, desire them. Associate with these qualities as they appear in the lives of great men. Let me give you a part of the account of Mr. Hubbard's "visit" with Horatio Nelson. Horatio was a poor sickly orphan boy who became one of the most important men of his day. How did he do it? Rest assured there was a *reason* for his greatness. See if you can find it and use it. And remember — what you desire, you may have; it will be sent to you free of charge.

Horatio Nelson was born in England in 1758. He went to sea as a stow-away at the age of twelve. It was a rough life for a small boy, but he had a way of rising to meet situations. Horatio decided he would do his job better than anyone else. He resolved to be the best seaman in the British Navy.

Mr. Hubbard says of him: "His quickness in obeying orders, his alertness and ability to climb, his scorn of danger, going to the yardarm to adjust a tangled rope in a storm, or fastening the pennant to the mast in less time than anyone else on board could perform the task, made him a marked man. He did the difficult thing, the unpleasant thing, with an amount of good cheer that placed him in a class by himself. He had no competition. Success was in his blood. His silent sober ways intent only on doing his duty, made his services sought after by every captain who was fitting out a ship for a dangerous undertaking." These qualities would have made him successful in any undertaking.

### His Rise

Nelson made a trip to the Arctic and came back a second mate at age nineteen. He was a lieutenant at twenty, a lieutenant commander at twenty-one, a captain at twenty-three, in charge of his own ship. On one occasion the Prince of Denmark came aboard his ship and asked for the captain. The Prince says, "I was shown a boy in a captain's uniform, the youngest man to look upon I ever saw holding a like position. But on talking with him, I saw he was a man who knew what he was doing."

From 1793 to 1798, Nelson made history and made it rapidly. He was in constant pursuit of the enemy with no respite from danger night or day. When a ship mutinied, they placed Nelson in charge of it if he was within call. He once said to a sullen, mutinous crew, "Our enemies are there, and I depend upon you to follow me over the side and annihilate them. You shall accept no danger that I do not accept, no hardship shall be yours that shall not be mine. I need no promise from you that you will do your duty. I know you will. You believe in me and I in you — we are Englishmen, fighting our country's battles and so to your work, my men, to your work." The mutinous spirit melted away, for the men knew that if Nelson fought with them it would be for the privilege of getting at the enemy first. No officer ever carried out sterner discipline with his men or with himself, and none was more implicitly obeyed.

### The Loss of An Arm

Nelson was advanced step by step until he became Admiral of the Fleet. At the Battle of Santa Cruz, he led a night attack. Standing in the prow of a small boat, his right arm was shattered at the elbow. He insisted on going forward and continued to command, even though his sword arm was useless.

Finally the loss of blood forced his attendants to take him back to his ship for medical treatment. When he arrived, the surgeons were already busy caring for the other wounded. Seeing their commander, the surgeons rushed to his assistance. He ordered them back, declaring he would take a place in line and wait his turn and this he did. When his time arrived the surgeons saw that his arm was shattered and the whole right hand reduced to a pulp, and that amputation was the only thing. There were no anesthetics, and Nelson watched the surgeons sever the worthless arm.

As they bandaged the stump he dictated a report of the battle to his secretary, but after writing for ten minutes the poor secretary fell in a faint and Nelson ordered one of the surgeons to complete taking the dictation. The final report contained no mention of the calamity that had befallen the commander. He regarded the loss of an arm as merely an incident in the great cause of winning his country's battles.

### Trumphant Return

In six months he had met and defeated all of the ships of Napoleon that could be located. When he returned to England, an ovation met him such as never before had been given to a seaman. He walked with a limp. No one knew for sure whether it was because they had pinned on him so many medals, or as someone else said, the limp may have been caused by undiscovered lead that had been shot into his body. But what is visible to the eye is not always the most important part of a great man.

Mr. Hubbard must have thrilled at the story of this orphan boy's climb to the post of Admiral of the British Fleet. The stunning success which flowed to Horatio Nelson was the result of his single-minded devotion to duty. He desired to be the best — he got what he desired.

And we should always remember in all our endeavers the fundamental principle of the Law of Attraction,: "Whatever we desire, we will get."

## Plans and Goals

# 27
# The Law of
# SELF-SUPERVISION

One of the curiosities of the human personality is that only a relatively few people ever learn to direct their own efforts according to their own previously thought-out plans. Many experiments have shown that if you have a five-man job to be done, it can be accomplished more quickly if you make one person the boss and hold him responsible for keeping the other four busy.

The amount of supervision a person requires largely determines what he or she is worth. If he requires a lot of supervision, he gets one amount; if he requires a little less supervision, he gets a little larger income; and when he can be depended upon to do his job without any supervision, he is worth still more. Of course, at the top of the list is the person who does his own work, on his own initiative, following his own plans which he himself has drawn and initiated, and who in addition stimulates others. He is the one who receives the top income.

## Only a Few Succeed

The tremendous expense involved in supervision is one of the heaviest burdens borne by our civilization. It is one of the great wastes in government, in church work, and in business affairs. Too often the initiative, the motivation, the reminding, the pep talks, and the planning must be provided for those who are unable to do those things for themselves. An interesting set of figures was recently released by the United States government that indicates this shortcoming in people. People are generally divided into three groups as follows:

 2 percent:  Work, manage, plan
14 percent: Work, manage
84 percent: Work

No matter what the job to be done may be, most people can learn how to do the actual work involved. Take, for example, the job of a farmer. Most normal persons can learn to plow, plant, cultivate, irrigate, and fertilize. Yet only a few ever become successful farmers. Why? Eighty-four percent can do the work all right, but that's all they can do. When the boss leaves, they sit down. They never learn to manage themselves and operate under their own supervision. Fourteen percent can do the work, and they can also manage themselves. When the supervisor is not present, these workers, unlike the 84 percent, do not quit. They keep going whether the boss is present or not. They not only do more work but also save the cost of their own supervision. In addition, someone must plan their work for them — the 2 percent at the top. They can work, they can manage themselves, and they can also plan.

It Takes Initiative

It is fine to be able to do important work skillfully and properly. And yet that is probably the smallest part of success. There are probably few salesmen, for example, who could not easily double their income. They could easily learn all of the steps involved in planning, prospecting, pre-approach, direct mail, approach, interviewing, answering objections, closing the sale, and so forth. It isn't the work that bothers us; it's learning to supervise and motivate ourselves — to think, to organize, and to execute our plans on our own power.

Most people, if left to their own devices, either sit down

or lie down or fall down on the job. The executive part of their personalities is nonproductive. The initiative and ability to keep going seem to have been ironed out of their personalities, and the planning ability has dried up in their minds.

This is a quality of partial nonproductiveness that is seen in nature. For example, Bing and Lambert cherry trees are incapable of producing fruit if left by themselves. They have no fertilizing pollen, and so a pollinizer must be planted among them. Then the wind and the bees carry the pollen to those trees that are incapable of self-fertilization.

Many people are like that with regard to work. One might be an excellent workman but not a self-starter. His initiative, ability to supervise, and ability to plan remain unproductive. Even though the necessary supervision is costly, such a worker must pay the heavy price and have someone stand over him and keep him going.

## To Fulfill Our Destiny

Elbert Hubbard was thinking about this situation when he said, "I am looking out through the library window into the apple orchard, and I see millions of blossoms that will never materialize and become fruit for lack of vitalization." The destiny of an apple blossom is that it should become an apple, and the destiny of a human soul is that it may become even as God. But neither of these things happen unless that vitalizing element is introduced that makes us productive.

*The highest classification of effort is exerted by the person who can work on his own power and who can also motivate others. He usually determines his own pay.*

In the process of training ourselves for success, we mustn't forget the importance of learning to stand on our own feet without always having to have someone there to prop us up, supply our ideas, and motivate us. One may be an excellent salesman, but if he doesn't know how to organize his time and is not capable of continuous effort on his own power, he allows this deficiency to iron the zeal out of his mind and immobilize his ambition until he becomes comparatively nonproductive.

## The Advantages of Self-supervision

There are many advantages in learning self-supervision, including the following:

1. Our pay is increased.
2. We get the kind of supervision we like best, which is our own. The best motivation always comes from the inside. When we have to have others supervise us, we often get someone whose personality does not harmonize with ours. If he is the supervisor, we must follow his ideas rather than our own. Frequently we do our work grudgingly because we resent our supervisor.
3. Many people in many kinds of work are not able to manage themselves, but instead of buckling in and learning how to discipline themselves, they quit their jobs and go to work for someone else. The newness of the supervision satisfies them for a while, but it isn't long before they again feel the temptation to jump to something else.
4. One of the most thrilling things in the world is to work for ourselves, to plan our own work, develop our own ideas, and be our own person. This is also the way to growth and happiness.

Success lies largely in the ability to handle ourselves. One of the most exalting feelings one will ever know is the feeling that he is bigger than circumstances and that he can stand on his own feet and make his own way against all obstacles. We reach this point by learning something that most people never find out: the art of self-supervision. Then we are bigger than anything that can happen to us.

# Plans and Goals

# 28
# The Law of
# EGO RECOGNITION

We have been given a natural urge to repeat those experiences which give us pleasure, and nature has provided that the greatest pleasure that ever comes to human beings is the one that comes as a reward of accomplishment. When we go to school, we would rather get A's than D's. When we get married, we would rather be put upon the pedestal than out in the dog house. When we are employed, we would rather be praised and promoted than kicked and fired. This is a natural law of our being, for we all want to be recognized and well spoken of.

Through the desire for approval and accomplishment, nature entices us onward and upward and thereby anticipates and provides for our improvement. This universal desire for reputation and approval excites and strengthens our passion for excellence. It creates helpful rivalry and productive, individual initiative.

### Natures Bribe

This natural tendency to be well thought of has been called the law of ego recognition. The ego is the most important part of a person. It is the seat of consciousness. It is the focal point of all the satisfactions. It is the center of pleasure, the "self." It is the general manager of our lives.

This power is strongest and most constructive when it is activated and used. By this process, nature "bribes" us to do things that are praiseworthy. The most distasteful of life's relations come when people do not approve of us and when we feel that our lives themselves are not worthwhile. On the other hand, nothing is really more delightful than the return of affection and a substantial feeling of esteem.

The ego is with us the day we are born and begins to show itself very early in life. In earliest infancy children cry to get attention. Later they develop all kinds of pranks to show themselves off favorably before others.

## We Hunger For Approval

Think about how this tendency works throughout our lives for our improvement. We do not wear particular and distinctive clothing merely to keep us warm and dry, but we choose color, style, padding, and whatnot for the purpose of being recognized and approved by other people. Our desires for education, to develop fine manners, culture, influence, power, come largely because of the hunger to be approved of.

Even the accumulation of money is more often than not a manifestation of the ego. Usually people do not work merely to obtain luxury or ease or enough money to supply their needs, because if that were true, they would stop when these things were obtained. But most people work for money long after the actual need has been satisfied, because money in excess of the amount required for the necessities may be used to provide power, prestige, leadership, more attractive homes, late model automobiles, and other status symbols for themselves. These things may also be used to help others, to be able to put ourselves in the right social groups and be approved by those who, to us, are important.

## Attention If Not Approval

We should of course, be careful that we do not allow any distortions of ego recognition to take place. Sometimes when people are unable to get attention through worthy means, they use other means in trying to reach the same end. Criminals try to build up their power and status by theft and crime. Some people become arsonists or gangsters to unlawfully get a feeling of importance and power. Instead of making themselves attractive, some go to the other extreme in dressing in ludicrous clothing, tearing down the establishment, and using other unlawful and improper methods of getting attention.

Our responsibility is to learn to understand the powerful law of ego recognition so that we can use it more effectively. If we can recognize this personality need in other people, we will be far more capable and effective in dealing with them as well as promoting our own interests by being worthy of approval by ourselves and others. But of even greater importance, we can use it in controlling ourselves.

Inertia, that tendency that we all have to "remain at rest," is one of the strongest negative powers in human beings, and we can use the thirst for recognition in ourselves to counteract this damaging influence.

## Using Our Own Egos to Build Success

Suppose we make a list of some of the things we might do to develop ourselves in the important success dimension.

1. We should always be very careful of our appearance and grooming, for these are powerful factors in the judgements others form of us. Cleanliness is next to godliness, and our personal and public acceptance is greatly influenced by our physical and moral cleanliness.

2. All of the qualities making for effectiveness, such as planning, industry, study, and our personal relations with people, give that feeling of contentment and satisfaction which feeds this important quality.

3. We ought to make ourselves competitive so we become worthy of our share of the respect and esteem of others. An ambition to excel in worthiness and accomplishment is indispensable to success.

4. We should be constantly alert to our own self improvement and the service of others.

5. Inasmuch as we all like to be identified with good things, we ought to associate ourselves with worthwhile undertakings, community work, church service, and being helpful to others.

6. Good public and personal relations are vital.

### Do Not Depend On Others For Recognition

We often make the great mistake of depending upon others for the recognition we crave. Many of life's failures excuse themselves on the grounds that their bosses or their spouses or someone else was not thoughtful enough to give all the pats and praises necessary for their motivation. It is, of course, fortunate when people are considerate and helpful, but why trust something as important as our own esteem to others who more likely than not will forget?

Suppose someone does forget us? Are we going to allow ourselves to be shipwrecks merely because others were not thoughtful? Many really great men, in certain periods of their lives, have been unappreciated. Many great discoverers, inventors, prophets, and social workers have not been given credit for what they have done. Even when praise is not forthcoming, it is silly to go into a tailspin and throw away our chances in life merely because someone was not properly interested in us.

The law of self-preservation requires that *we* provide the substance on which we ourselves will survive. We don't expect someone else to be responsible for providing our food, our health, our muscles, and all the other qualities necessary for our survival. We must develop the abilities and skills to get these things for ourselves. To merely sit back and hope that somebody else will supply them for us is unwise, and we will soon find ourselves in difficulty if we depend upon it.

Earn Your Own Approval

Why should we not also provide for ourselves the things required by this companion instinct of ego recognition? We know when our conduct is praiseworthy. We can do the things that will give to ourselves satisfaction, peace of mind, and the knowledge of acomplishment far more satisfying than any pat on the back that might come from someone who is not as interested in our success as we ourselves are.

Robert Louis Stevenson said, "I know what pleasure is, for I have done good work." The highest enjoyment is that of being content with ourselves. Meissonier never worried very much about pleasing other people. He said, "I have someone who is more difficult to please than you. I must satisfy myself." And usually, if we really earn our own approval, we will also have the appreciation of others.

# Plans and Goals

# 29
# The Law of
# PRACTICE

It has been said that practice makes perfect. What we do not always remember is that that may be our undoing. A man who practices being grouchy with his family and friends gives a permanent form to his personality.

One may practice being cynical or sarcastic in jest, or he may be vindictive and revengeful with his enemies, only to find that before he knows it, the cement has set and he has unintentionally become something that will be unprofitable to himself and to everyone else.

One's posture, attitudes, expressions or thoughts grow rapidly, the malignant as well as the good, the mental as well as the physical. We become worriers by worrying; we become idlers by idling; we become successful thinkers by thinking successfully, crooked thinkers by thinking crookedly.

## Practice Can Make Mediocre

Practice, drill, repetition, good or bad, make us what we are. A stenographer may write 80 words per minute upon graduation from business college; then after three years of continual practice she takes another test and finds that she can now only do 50 words per minute. Her practice has been wrong. Or here is a boy practicing throwing a basketball. He loves to handle the ball and he does it just for fun, and is not concerned whether or not it goes through the hoop; he therefore practices throwing the ball inaccurately to his own hurt.

The golfer who becomes a champion is the one who plays every stroke as though he were in the tournament where everything is counted. One who is not concerned about his occupation becomes mediocre because of his mediocre practice. What we practice in our leisure time is just as important as what we practice on the job. Our subconscious mind is not aware when we are practicing or when we are performing.

It is often true that when we are on vacation or out of sight of our friends, we tend to let down to our detriment. When we are not on parade and when we do a different kind of thing than when we are at our best we are making progress backward. We often lose quickly, by negligence, what it took us many years to build up by painstaking effort. We gather such a heavy weight of bad habits that our problems become too unwieldy for those forces that animate them.

### Gangster or Patriot?

For a young boy to play at being a gangster in his leisure time is quite different than playing at being a patriot. It's only in fun, but when we practice, everything counts at face value. Your subconscious mind has no way of telling when you are only playing. The chain of habit is too light to be felt until it is too strong to be broken. No one can afford to be slipshod, evasive, or hypocritical whether in work or play.

When one acts as though he wants to be a "nobody," nature assumes he is in earnest and grants his wish. No one can afford to shirk, or make-believe or practice pretense in any action of life because all of the time he is molding himself into a deformity and shifting away from the divine.

Jesus said, "Love your enemies." Why? Because to practice hating anyone is very bad business. If you practice loving your enemies, you ought to be in pretty good form when it comes to loving your friends. It was also said that we should "return good for evil" for the same reason and that is — we need the practice. We do in jest many things we would not think of doing seriously. But we had better watch out. Confucius said, "Jest not over holy matters." That is good psychology. The Law of Practice has no way of knowing the difference, the recording device is never turned off, and so everything goes into the personality to make us what we are.

## Curing Habits

A habit is like some diseases. In the beginning it is easy to cure, but hard to recognize; whereas after a time if not detected and treated, it becomes easy to recognize but difficult to cure.

All the energy we have is needed in our business and anyone who starts out on the wrong path, finds himself treading upon brambles and nettles that will close in behind him and make his return impossible. Every minute of our lives we are practicing something — how we walk, sit, think, feel. The secret of success is to practice only things that will improve us.

## Aspiring to Greatness

We ought to practice time control, thought control, health control, habit control, feeling control, and never allow ourselves for one minute to practice those things which will be harmful to us. One who aspires to be great in any field should think about being great twenty-four hours a day. Those people who take a "vacation" in which they let down and practice bad habits had better beware. Our success is determined by what we practice in and out of season. One can't be great on the stage if he practices the wrong things off stage.

No one can harm us but ourselves and until someone invents a method of turning off our personality recording device when we want a vacation, we had better be careful.

Practice is a wonderful device by which we can make ourselves a champion in any field we may choose. It is an exciting idea to contemplate to what great heights this one thing may lift us.

# Plans and Goals

# 30
# The Law of
# APPRECIATION

Two sections make up the law of appreciation. One is to be sincerely sympathetic with an understanding of other people; the other is never to count too much on appreciation for ourselves no matter how deserving we may be. We should remember everything that everyone does for us, but we should quickly forget that which we do for them.

## Gratitude A Virtue

One of the strongest hungers in human beings is the desire to be appreciated. Everyone wants to be liked. No one wins the esteem of another quite so quickly as the one who feels and shows appreciation for others. There should be genuine regard for every good thing that the other person is and does. Cicero said that "gratitude is the mother of virtues." Gratitude is also the sign of a noble soul. It always draws out the best in others. It always pays the largest dividends. To give appreciation is one of the best and easiest ways to gain power.

One of the serious weaknesses in human character is the fact that people so often fail to give appreciation to other people as the other people think they should be appreciated. One outstanding example is the lack of appreciation in children. One father can support ten children, but who has ever seen ten children who were able to support one father? If we loan a man money when he is broke, almost always he becomes an enemy and, in addition, he is reluctant to repay the money unless we foreclose his home or hurt him bad enough in some other way. Try it if you don't believe it. Do someone a favor and see what happens.

We know of thousands of cases where an employer has taken a young man into his business or home, taught him his business, financed and helped him, and then, after the young man has learned all the secrets of the business, he becomes the benefactor's most bitter competitor.

Judas was given high position by Jesus, yet Judas betrayed his greatest benefactor for thirty pieces of silver — about $13 in today's currency.

Appreciation Is Rare

It is, of course, not true that people never show appreciation for the good that is done them. Jesus found ten men stricken with the dreaded disease of leprosy, which had made them unfit for the society of other men. It is difficult to imagine men in a worse situation; yet, after Jesus healed all of them, only one of the ten came back to say thank you.

Many would say that one out of ten is a pretty good average. This story is a good one because if one out of twelve betrays us and one out of ten comes around to express appreciation we are doing as well as did the greatest man who ever lived. In fact, the entire life story of Jesus, including his death, illustrates this fundamental trait in human personality. The greatest benefactor of men who ever lived suffered the most cruel death at the hands of the very people he was trying to benefit. This is not just an isolated case. It is a common weakness in human personality.

Because we are all hungry for recognition, our situation becomes particularly dangerous if we allow ourselves to expect appreciation when the chances are so great that we will not get it. It does not matter why lack of appreciation is so prevalent in human nature. It is enough to know that it is true. Someone has said, "When I do right no one remembers, and when I do wrong no one forgets."

Sometimes persons with a great desire to do good suffer disappointment after disappointment, for not only are they not appreciated, but they actually receive abuse as their pay. Not understanding that this is a common weakness in men sometimes tends to make them bitter and to ruin their lives. They draw into themselves and quit bestowing favors inasmuch as their last attempts were unappreciated or even boomeranged to hurt them.

### Withdrawal Is Disastrous

Withdrawl is the most disastrous course to follow, for the one who withdraws from his fellows is the one who is hurt most. The solution is to eliminate the expectation of praise or appreciation as a motive in our behavior. When we do anything, the criteria to depend on is whether it is right or wrong, not whether or not we expect commendation for it. Then we control the situation in our own minds, and we always receive satisfaction from our good deeds when we have control of the situation. If one out of ten comes to thank us, we are just that much ahead of the game and feel doubly repaid, but if everyone forgets or even turns against us, we will not be disappointed, because we had not counted on it anyway.

The old saying, "Expect nothing and you will never be disappointed," may seem harsh, but it does contain some good logic. We have occasionally seen those people who do everything they do in the hope of receiving praise; and they are always unhappy and disappointed, because in nine cases out of ten, they just do not receive the praise they sought. That is not the way a human being is put together.

### The Public Is Fickle

A public servant may serve his country faithfully for a lifetime, but because of some little thing, because the wind blows temporarily from another direction, all the good is forgotten. The public is said to be fickle. Everyone has a short memory of other people's virtues or good deeds. It may be too bad, but just remember it is often so.

It is much better philosophy to remember that the greatest person is the one who confers the most benefits, whether anyone remembers or not. We should remember also that it is difficult for others to see with our eyes and understand with our understanding. There will naturally be differences of opinion of our good deeds. It is not likely that one's companions will value him at the same value he sets on himself. We should be prepared for this in advance. We can just as well learn to think kindly of people even when they do not give us credit. It is a practical application of the old story of returning good for evil. This is a great philosophy for happiness, and it is sound to the core. We must learn to serve if we want to progress. We should have the attitude of always doing more than we get paid for. Just think how much good we could do if we didn't care who got the credit.

## Learn to Serve

A good motto to keep in mind is that people who expect gratitude for everything they do really do not deserve gratitude. The history of the world has shown that beneficiaries usually have short memories, and benefactors seldom receive proper appreciation. Moses, like many other great men, suffered most at the hands of his friends. He was the object of continual murmurings by the people he had given his life to serve.

One of the greatest dangers one can place himself in is to take the same attitude toward his benefactors that he does toward his beneficiaries. The law of appreciation says that we should develop great gratitude toward the one and not expect too much from the others. In that way, everyone will be happy, and after all, what difference does it make? We must learn to serve if we want to progress. We should have the attitude of always doing more than we get paid for. Whether we agree with this element in human nature or not is of little importance. All that matters is that we understand and obey the law.

# Plans and Goals

# 31
# The Law of
# FINANCIAL RESPECTABILITY

Many otherwise good men allow success to elude them because they lack financial respectability. It is not uncommon to see men who are well developed in other parts of their personalities but who lack good financial sense. In human relations, few qualities make one so vulnerable to defeat as the quality of not knowing how to handle oneself financially. One may be weak in some parts of one's personality without interfering with success in other areas, but one who is financially insecure has a difficult time in most other areas of life. Someone said, "I am not sure just what the unpardonable sin is, but I believe it is the disposition to postpone and evade the payment of one's bills."

Probably few things could be more helpful in developing our religion, our morality, our citizenship, and our own morale than sound financial maturity. A book has been written entitled *How Old Am I Financially?* If we can answer this question, we can fortell much of our own future. It is suggested that each human being should review his financial habits so that they will not hold him back without his knowing it. Here are some suggestions to help us do this.

Financial Habits to Form

1. *Develop the habit of paying promptly for what you get.*

There are, of course, cases when installment payments may be all right, but some people want to give us credit when we don't need it, and everyone is suspicious of a person when he is broke.

Through the process of unbusiness-like conduct, creditors sometimes wear themselves out with waiting and promises. What kind of impression does that make? Just think of the person who borrows money and then makes the lender come back again and again, begging and coaxing to get what belongs to him, and then pays it in little hand-outs over an extended period.

If a person needs more money, there is one good way to get it, and that is to do more and better work. If we always practice spending less than we earn, we will usually have a surplus. But no matter to whom we owe money, we should always be sure payment is made promptly before it is due, or if we cannot make payment, we are the ones who should do the worrying about it. A borrower can make a fine name for himself by going out of his way to let his creditors know that he is on the job and working in their interests.

2. *Shakespeare gave some excellent advice when he said:*

> *Neither a borrower, nor a lender be,*
> *For a loan oft loses both itself and friend,*
> *And borrowing dulls the edge of husbandry.*

*It is dangerous to borrow money from friends or associates.* Some people spend more time trying to "work their friends" for loans than it would take to earn the needed money; and, of course, people who borrow from or loan to their friends put their friendship in great jeopardy.

3. *Develop financial integrity.*

Some people who are otherwise considered honest develop sneaky little financial habits. They try to "chisel" on a deal after it has been made. They "welch" on their word. They promise but when the time arrives, they put us off.

They seem to completely disregard our pleasure and convenience. They have a lot of excuses, but they don't pay. They like to eat if someone else will pay the check. An attitude of trying to get something for nothing is very bad business and usually backfires with disastrous results.

### 4. *Build a financial reserve.*

No one would think of starting to drive across a desert in his automobile without a spare tire. No one would feel entirely safe on a dangerous ocean voyage without a lifeboat. Just so, every human being ought to have a substantial financial life preserver in the form of a sizable reserve. Having money in the bank gives a person a spirit of self-confidence. It builds determination, self-reliance, self-respect, self-control. A reserve is one of the best weapons for the conquest of fear.

### 5. *Have adequate life insurance protection.*

Every man who gets married and brings children into the world should have an adequate life insurance program to provide them with financial responsibility in the event of his death.

### 6. *Use personal credit wisely.*

In everyone's life there sometimes come emergencies when extra money is needed. Some people solve this problem by (a) letting their bills go, thus inconveniencing those with whom they do business; or (b) borrowing little dabs of others' money on a friendship basis from personal acquaintances.

Both of these methods tear down one's public relations and peace of mind. A person of sound financial sense will establish his credit so he is prepared for emergencies long before they happen. The financial institutions with which he has done business in the past should have absolute confidence in his ability to earn, his integrity in meeting his obligations promptly, and his absolute honesty. He never tries to cut corners. He never disappoints anyone. He is never late and never makes his creditors remind him that the payment is overdue.

### 7. *Develop a sense of community responsibility.*

A part of everyone's financial education should be the recognition of his responsibility to the community in which he lives, not just by paying his taxes — in that he has no choice — not in just doing his part of church and community work. The person who feels that the world owes him a living always has an unhappy time trying to collect it. However, the one who feels that the welfare of the community is his responsibility will get his contribution back increased many fold. Part of all one earns should be put back into the community, just as a good farmer reserves his best grain to seed the soil out of which his profits come.

### 8. *Establish financial respectability at home.*

An easy place to take one's own financial measure is to check up on how one handles himself financially in his own home. Some men compel their wives to beg and bribe and crawl and plead for money. Others give them a definite allowance each month. Some of the advantages to this latter procedure may be as follows:

a. The wife becomes the financial manager in the home. She pays the bills, looks after the details, oversees the shopping, and leaves the husband's time free for one of his major responsibilities, which is to earn the money.

b. She is thereby trained in handling money, which is of great value to her now and in the future. She learns to stand alone on her own financial feet, which may be of great value should future circumstances make that necessary. Some men fail in this area because their minds are cluttered up with a thousand little distractions and side issues that could be much more efficiently handled by the wife.

c. She develops more interest in the business and economy of the home as well as in the business from which the income is received when she is an interested partner rather than when someone else makes all of the financial decisions.

d. She has a definite income so that she can make plans and use her intelligence for the welfare of the unit.

## How to Have Peace of Mind in Your Work

Now, suppose there isn't always enough money to go around. No one always has an income and an outgo that exactly fit each other every month. Emergencies sometimes throw a large, unlooked-for expense into the debit side of the monthly budget. How a man handles his wife financially may indicate how he handles other people. It's pretty hard to be one thing in one's own home and something else elsewhere.

Now think of another man who sends his check to the bank and the bank automatically deposits the agreed-upon amount in the wife's account. He is the breadwinner and he bears the load that goes with that responsibility. Why should a person be more dependable with his creditors than he is with his own family? Irregular times will come, and so he should prepare for them in advance. Home is a good place to practice these major virtues. A wife above all other people should know that her husband can be absolutely depended upon and that her share of money will be in the bank not later than a couple of days before it is due.

Many divorces and hard feelings between husband and wife are concerned with finances, and not always with the amount. Often trouble arises because dependability and understanding of having everything done satisfactorily have not been worked out in advance. If people plan their affairs and then learn to be financially responsible, they seldom have to discuss finances. Few things build up good internal relations like financial understanding, confidence, and respectability. If you want peace of mind in your work, get financially organized at home.

## Shirking Doesn't Solve the Problem

There are some people who write checks that are not

covered by sufficient funds. In public relations this is close to suicide. It is also legal suicide in some cases. Everyone should learn to be a good financial planner. He should know how much money he needs and the amount of work necessary in order to produce it, and a little bit extra. Some people will go to almost any limit to keep from real, honest-to-goodness, productive work. They will lie down on the job, shirk responsibilities, dodge their creditors, jump their bills, borrow money from their friends, or even beg from their children. And then much of this is wasted on tobacco, liquor, gambling, and other sinful vices. Many people force their families to live second-class lives and endure all the other torments of being broke in order to avoid doing the things that make money and produce income. We become successful by design; we become shirkers, buck passers, and beggars by default.

Whether our income is large or small is not the point. The point is to do our best and learn to handle well what we have, so that everyone with whom we do business will receive genuine satisfaction from his contact with us. That way we ourselves will feel good about what we do. Someone said that we should always treat others as though we were the other. This is a wonderful idea. If we can learn to put it into practice, we will be really great human beings. Yes, one of the most important laws of success is the law of financial respectability.

## Plans and Goals

# 32
# The Law of
# SELF-DECEPTION

Since I was a child, I have heard that the ostrich buries his head in the sand when he is afraid, to hide from the danger that threatens him. I have asked several people who should know something about ostriches, and I am convinced that ostriches do not do this. Someone has maligned the poor bird by assigning to him a trait characteristic of certain human beings but not of ostriches. When an ostrich is frightened, he either fights or runs.

### Hiding From The Facts

However, think how this characteristic of trying to hide from our fears manifests itself in some people. In the movies when a woman is terribly frightened, she usually screams and covers her eyes with her hands so that she cannot see the horror or danger by which she is threatened. When a person is operated on, he closes his eyes so he cannot see himself get hurt. When we see a terrible accident, we turn our faces away so we cannot see it. To most unpleasant sights we close our eyes. When we smell something unpleasant, we hold our noses. When we hear something unpleasant, we put our fingers in our ears. When we think something unpleasant, we take a dose of sleeping pills or tranquilizers.

This trait of hiding from disagreeable facts is especially

manifest when someone is trying to make suggestions to help us. It is a paradox that the recipients of advice should feel no annoyance when they ought to feel some and yet feel so much when they ought not to. They are usually vexed not at all at having committed the fault, but very angry at being reproved for it.

One of the things that often holds us back in our success is the deliberate attempt we make to hide from the facts when the facts are unpleasant. Advice is seldom valued, though there is a great deal of advising and very little listening. Usually we do not want advice; we want flattery. And yet one cannot easily be our flatterer and our friend at the same time. Some people actually owe more to bitter enemies than to pleasant friends. The former sometimes speak the truth; the latter seldom do. An enemy is often a friend in disguise who stings us into action. He tells us the truth about ourselves. Cato asserted that wise men profit more from fools than fools do from wise men, for some wise men try to avoid the faults of fools, but fools seldom try to imitate the good examples of wise men.

## Learn to Look Critically At Yourself

There is a great book entitled *Damaged Souls,* written by Gamaliel Bradford, which is a series of biographies of near-great men who were prevented from becoming what their virtues intended because they also had accompanying faults. The author said that *there was no evidence that any one of the men ever developed the ability to stand off and look critically at himself.*

Some mental patients never look into themselves, into their way of living and thinking, in an effort to see whether their symptoms may be associated with their ways of living. The reason why they do not is obvious. They are not going to see what they do not want to see; they cannot be expected to destroy their defenses, and so many of these unfortunates are not even aware of their troubles.

Each human being is trusted with the responsibility of making an effective personality. Our judgment is no better than our information, and when we deliberately practice self-deception, our judgement becomes useless or actually harmful. Kings and other rulers are often particularly unfortunate. They are shut off and shielded from the truth on every side. They get their facts secondhand and are lied to all day long. Consequently they become in time incapable of digesting truth.

Most people have an epidermis that is too thin to stand criticism. What we usually want is salve — soft, pleasant, emolient, gracious salve. We demand praise, not suggestion. We wish to be saved from the mischief of our vices, not from the vices themselves.

Someone said, "Truly, it is an evil thing to be full of faults, but is is still a greater evil to be full of them and be unwilling to recognize them, since that is to add the further fault of voluntary delusion." *If you would escape vexation, reprove yourself liberally and others sparingly*. We do not like others to deceive us. We do not think it fair that they should be held in higher esteem by us than they deserve. Neither is it fair that we should deceive them or wish them to esteem us more highly than we deserve. But good or bad, almost the last thing anyone wants is counsel.

No criminal ever calls himself a criminal. Jesse James thought himself a benefactor to society. Napoleon said, "I believe I will be without parallel in history, that a plain man shall have attained to such amazing power without committing a single crime." All this, of course, is self-deception. It is a crime to deceive other people, and it is a calamity to deceive ourselves, especially when we go so far that it is often impossible to get ourselves undeceived.

Get A Coach

If you really wish to improve yourself, you need someone on the sidelines to coach you and to observe your mistakes and warn you against repetition. Without someone to tell you the truth about your annoying mannerisms and bad habits and inexcusable mistakes, you may fall into the pit of self-delusion where disaster lurks. Thus, for self-improvement, get a close friend to tell you off occasionally. He will act as a mirror in which you can see yourself as others see you.

Criticism is the hardest medicine to take, but it keeps us awake, while the kindness of a courteous friend is an opiate that puts us to sleep. The "yes man" seldom gives any constructive help. This is an area where even an enemy might be helpful, because he may be vulgar enough and merciless enough to say the things about us that will enable us to rid ourselves of our most serious shortcomings. And, of course, a wise person will listen instead of fighting back. This inability to learn the truth about ourselves is a stumbling block on which we often fall and break the necks of our personalities and our success.

Look Within

Each of us should at least be aware of the tendency within us to hide from the facts, and every effective person should develop the ability to look within himself.

One of the medical sciences is called vivisection, by which a doctor cuts into living tissues — not to kill, but to study the workings of vital organs so he can find out and cure the hidden trouble. A kind of vivisection — or mental introspection — for ourselves is just as important, and if we do not master the process by practice, it may be just about as traumatic to cut into our personalities as it would be to cut into our abdomens.

Everyone ought to have an employer or a marriage partner or a religious counselor or a trusted friend who can cut into the tissues of his attitudes and habits occasionally, not to kill him but to bring him back to life. It's easy to see faults from the sidelines, but everyone has a blind spot where he himself is concerned. If we are so fortunate as to have someone who will occasionally give us the facts about our problems, we shouldn't get angry at him. We should listen and keep our heads out of the sand and our eyes and ears open.

We should never deceive our friends, but even more important, we should not deceive ourselves.

# Plans and Goals

# 33
# The Law of
# FUSION

Did you ever find a tiny fly in a great bowl of soup? What was your reaction? One thing is certain: *all* of the soup was spoiled.

Now think of a young man of good character associating with men of questionable reputation. What is the verdict? The law says, "You are judged by the company you keep." The part is merged with and judged by the whole. Also, the whole is judged by the part. That is the law of fusion.

Many times we don't separate values, but allow them to run together. They fuse into one another. The personality of the part takes on the character of the whole. If the gummed paper that is stuck full of dead flies in the butcher shop window is in the same area as a steak we might want for dinner, the whole becomes one. It is a little difficult to think of them separately. This is the law of fusion. This is one of the reasons why good merchants dare not mix cheap merchandise with that which is expensive. The price tags are different, but our impressions associate them together, and the good merchandise is spoiled by being too close to the bad.

### The Impression We Make

Now think of our personality qualities. Our personalities are the sum total of our characters, our appearance, our attitudes, our habits, our skills, and our spiritual qualities, which distinquish us from all others. The clothes we wear, the lines in our faces, the tone of our voices, the thoughts we think, the character we have developed by those thoughts, the expression of our eyes, the attractive smile, the magnetic handshake, the company we represent, the friends we associate with — all constitute a part of our personality. We may have fifty personality traits, but we make only one impression.

Now suppose one has a dirty collar or dirty fingernails or some other annoying mannerism or personality fault. What is the result likely to be? Probably the same as the flypaper in the butcher shop window. A chain is no stronger than its weakest link, and our entire personality may be neutralized by some small defect. One tiny spot of rot in a great apple not only classifies the whole apple as rotten, but also endangers all of the other apples nearby.

We are very fortunate if we have a friend who is wise enough and courageous enough to sit down with us occasionally and point out our weak points before this deadly law does too much damage. And we are even more fortunate if we will listen and take heed. Even our appraisal by an enemy is sometimes more accurate than our appraisal of ourselves.

### Is There A Dead Mouse Around?

Every person should have some machinery set up for an occasional self-analysis where he attempts to see himself as others see him. What about our speech and our honesty? Are we pulled down by a personality millstone around our necks? Do we have a "dead mouse" in our personality? If we have, the law of fusion will relegate us to a position in the rear of the procession toward success. Remember this: the weak and the strong, the rich and the poor, the ignorant and the well-informed are changing places continually, and whether we are going up or coming down, whether we are eliminating or acquiring defects, and whether this law of fusion will work for us or against us should be a matter of daily and earnest concern.

An important part of a strong physical body is a well-regulated elimination system whereby the waste and impurities are regularly being expelled. That is just as necessary to a vigorous, alert, healthy personality. Remember the law of fusion. The whole is judged by the part, and the part is judged by the whole.

# Plans and Goals